PASTOR, I AM GAY

To Peggy —
Until there is Shalom!

Howard Bess

PASTOR, I AM GAY

by the Rev. Howard H. Bess

Palmer Publishing Company
P.O. Box 3938, Palmer, Alaska 99645

Scripture quotations are from the New Revised Standard Version Bible, Copyright 1989, by the Division of Christian Education of the National Council of Churches of Christ in the United States of America. Used by permission.

Book design and cover art by Martha Gustafson Rozkydal.

First Edition 1995.
Second printing

Published by Palmer Publishing Company, Palmer, Alaska

Printed by A.T. Publishing and Printing, Inc.
Anchorage, Alaska.

Printed in the United States of America.

* * * * : *

LIBRARY OF CONGRESS CATALOG-IN-PUBLICATION DATA
Bess, Howard H. (Howard Hartzell), 1928-
    Pastor, I am gay / by the Rev. Howard H. Bess. — 1st ed.
        p. cm.
    Includes bibliographical references
    ISBN 0-9644123-0-6 (pbk.)
    1. Homosexuality—Religious aspects—Christianity. 2.
Homosexuality—Religious aspects—Baptists. 3. Church work with
gays—United States. 4. Church work with gays—Baptists. 5. Bess, Howard
H. (Howard Hartzell), 1928-   . 6. American Baptist Churches in the
U.S.A.—Doctrines. 7. Gay men—United States—Religious life. 8.
Lesbians—United States—Religious life. 9. Reconciliation—Religious
aspects—Christianity. 10. Reconciliation—Religious aspects—Baptists. I.
Title. 241'.66—dc20
                                      94-47332
                                         CIP

TABLE OF CONTENTS

FOREWORD

William R. Herzog II

This is a book whose time has come, not just for American Baptists but for all Christians who value the church as a prophetic community rooted in the gospel of Jesus Christ. In each generation, different forms of oppression and injustice arise to challenge the church to be faithful to her calling, and in this generation, the leading issue may just be social justice for gay and lesbian people. Certainly, Howard Bess has made a persuasive argument that this should be the case. One thing is clear: a church that is willing to sacrifice its prophetic voice on this issue for the sake of a spurious church unity has sacrificed its claim to be the body of Christ in the world. As this book is published, American Baptists are in serious conflict over this issue. The Association of Welcoming and Affirming Churches is gathering and uniting congregations who are openly welcoming to gays and lesbians while other congregations are questioning their right to remain part of the American Baptist Churches precisely because of their stand on this issue. The conflict will grow more intense before it is resolved and threatens to divide the ABC. So this book could not be published at a more opportune time.

The great strength of this book is its variety and versatility. Part I traces the author's personal journey and evolving understanding of gay and lesbian people. Because his journey is typical of so many of us, it is an illuminating and compelling tale, far more than an idiosyncratic story. It is unfortunate that more of us who have made this sojourn have not reflected on it as honestly and helpfully as has Howard Bess. His story alone could provide grist for many discussion mills while provoking opportunities for others to disclose their stories as well.

The great strength of Part II is the time it devotes to introducing us to the stories of gay men and lesbian women. These stories are most important because they remind us that homosexuality is not an abstract issue to be debated but real people to be encountered. If oppression works best when the oppressed can be dehumanized and demonized, then these introductions do provide a significant antidote to the toxin of homophobia. Out of the friendships I have formed with gays and lesbians, I have come to realize that derogatory remarks directed at them are being directed at my friends, and I take offence at attacks on my friends.

Since the Bible has played such a crucial role in the condemnation of same gender sexuality, Bess devotes a short but pertinent chapter to the biblical texts most often cited. He combines pastoral wisdom with sound interpretive insights in his approach to these passages, and within the span of a few pages defuses the most explosive texts. In light of the work of biblical scholars and the recent denominational discussion conducted in the American Baptist Quarterly (Vol. XII, 4, Dec. 93) Bess's work stands on firm ground. The chapters devoted to the church's ministry could be published separately as a handbook for local congregations, filled as they are with specific suggestions on larger practical issues. This book represents the distillation of serious reflection over a long period of time, and the reader will benefit from it.

Having said all of this, I have still not touched the heart of this book. It is the courage of Howard Bess. I have known and admired Howard for many more years than either of us would care to acknowledge, and throughout those years, he has incarnated ministry at its best and embodied the courage of the prophet. A lesser soul would have sold out long ago and quietly filed the issue of same gender relations in the inactive file while pursuing his career. Not Howard Bess, and he has paid a price for his courage. This book bears the mark of his integrity on every page.

When he asked me if I would be willing to write this foreword, he was even thoughtful enough to give me an out. "If writing it puts you in jeopardy," he told me, "please feel free to decline the offer." This leads to my final point. The time has come to speak out, not keep silence. At the moment, I am speaking to my heterosexual friends, not to my gay and lesbian brothers and sisters. The time has come for us to come out of the closets of our silence and advocate for justice. Nothing less will do. The voices of oppression are strong just now and filled with a sense of the righteousness of their cause. The prophetic voice of the gospel of Jesus Christ is needed now more than ever, right now, on this issue. If not, we may relive the experience of Pastor Martin Niemoller, a German pastor in the confessing church in Germany during the years of the rise of Nazism. "When they came for the Jews," he wrote, "I didn't protest because I wasn't a Jew. And when they came for the Catholics, I didn't protest because I wasn't a Catholic. And when they came for the trade unionists, I didn't protest because I wasn't a member of a union. And when they came for the Communists, I didn't protest because I wasn't a Communist. And when they came for me there was no one left to protest." I want to stop the avalanche of hatred, bigotry and homophobia before they come for the first group on their list, which in our culture could well be gays and lesbians. I do not want my silence construed as support for violence, injustice and oppression.

We need a groundswell of gospel acceptance and love just now. We need to create communities of faith in which there is neither gay nor straight, neither male nor female, neither minority culture nor majority culture. As Paul said, "The same Lord is the Lord of all and is generous to all who call on him." (Romans 10:12) This is the Lord who broke down the dividing wall of hostility creating one new humanity which we call the church. Howard Bess has done a great service to Christ's church by writing this book, and I am honored to write this preface to his significant work.

William R. Herzog II is Vice President for Academic Life, Dean of Faculty, and Professor of New Testament Interpretation, The Divinity School, Rochester, New York.

PREFACE

The decision to write this book was made on Friday, February 1, 1991. I was attending a conference sponsored by my denomination, the American Baptist Churches of the USA in Carson, California. The theme of the conference was *Extending the Hand of Fellowship*. I am proud of my denomination because of its commitment to diversity. We were the first American predominately white denomination to elect a black president. We were also the first major church body to choose a woman as our presiding officer. We supported the abolition of slavery, the underground railroad, and national reconciliation after the Civil War ended.

We work hard on the side of equal rights and opportunities for all minority groups. We advocate equality in church membership, housing, education, employment, voting, and public accommodations. Each year we sponsor the settlement of more immigrant people than any other Protestant body. The *Extending the Hand of Fellowship* conference was an exercise in maintaining our skills in the welcoming of diversity in our churches. It was a good conference.

When I received the conference materials, I noted that no place had been made in the program to face the challenge of welcoming gay and lesbian persons into our congregations. The first day of the conference I talked with Owen Owens, the denominational executive who had primary responsibility for planning the conference. My question to him was simple: "Why are we not facing the challenge of welcoming gay and lesbian persons into our congregations?" His answer was honest and to the point. "The planning committee did discuss the subject, but decided that we were not yet ready to face the issue." To me, it was the same answer people had tried to give to the black equal rights issue in the 1960s. Just be patient. We know what is right. We will deal with the matter later.

I went on my way, hardly satisfied.

On Thursday evening my passions were stirred. The preacher for the evening was a prominent black minister who preached a magnificent sermon. The Gospel knows nothing of barriers. It is good news for everyone. The response of the conference attendees was enthusiastic. The sermon called forth my own heartfelt "amens." It was the closing hymn, however, that stirred me most. The hymn was the familiar "For Those Tears I Died" by Marsha Stevens. Three things struck me: First the hymn was mimeographed in its entirety, probably in violation of copyright laws. Second, I noted that the name of the author had been omitted; that was probably a secretarial error. Third, I knew the story of Marsha Stevens, a very gifted lesbian Christian musician. She is the unacknowledged author of the song.

The song was written when Marsha was sixteen years of age. She had come to realize that she was lesbian. Rejected by family and church, her life had become unbearably painful, and she was contemplating suicide. In her pain Marsha took a leap of faith and believed that God loved her and accepted her just as she was. In that circumstance Marsha wrote her first song: "And Jesus said 'come to the waters, stand by my side.'" When the song is placed in its author's context, it surges with power.

The ironies that night were overpowering for me. A conference that had specifically decided not to welcome homosexuals openly was singing the song of one of the unwelcome ones. They left her name off the song, leaving it faceless. They did feel free to reproduce the song without appropriate permission. I stewed all night. I ate lunch the next day with two of my ministerial colleagues. I shared with them my feelings and frustrations. One of them asked me what I was going to do about it. I decided to write a book.

10

A NOTE ABOUT THE CLOSET

In writing *Pastor, I Am Gay* I faced one of the great ethical commitments which is respected and honored among gay men and lesbians. IT IS NEVER OKAY FOR ANYONE TO TAKE A GAY MAN OR LESBIAN OUT OF THEIR CLOSET. The task is theirs alone. To avoid taking anyone out of the closet, I have fictionalized many stories. I have changed the location of events. I have changed names. I have changed people's professions. I have made a concerted effort to record faithfully the basic dynamics of people's lives without opening their personal closet doors.

I look forward to the day when hiding will no longer be a necessity for gay men and lesbians in order for them to live, work, worship, play, and enjoy their God given lives. I pray this writing project will make a contribution to the end of the era of the closet.

Howard H. Bess

INTRODUCTION

I am an American Baptist pastor. From the time of my calling to be a pastor, I have never wanted to be anything other than a pastor. I have pastored American Baptist Churches for thirty-six years. I can identify no reason for writing this book other than my concerns as a pastor for persons who happen to be gay or lesbian. Neither of my parents was homosexual. None of my brothers and sisters are homosexual. None of my children are homosexual. I am a heterosexual who has enjoyed his sexuality. But the challenge of being a pastor, as I understand it, is to be a helper of persons regardless of their personal circumstances. If it is true that Christ died for all, pastors have no basis on which to exclude persons who are gay or lesbian from pastoral embrace.

I am a graduate of Wheaton College. I started my learning about human growth and development under Dr. Mary LeBarr at Wheaton. The subject of homosexuality was never raised to my recollection. My introduction to psychology was under Dr. Philip Marquart, a psychiatrist who taught in Wheaton's psychology department. Again I have no recollection of discussion of the homosexual phenomenon.

My seminary training took me first to Northern Baptist Theological Seminary in Chicago. I studied there for two full years. I have no recollection of any mention of the subject of homosexuality. I transferred in 1956 to Garrett Biblical Institute (now Garrett Evangelical Theological Seminary) on the campus of Northwestern University in Evanston, Illinois. I transferred for only one reason. Dr. Carol Wise was on the Garrett faculty and was a pioneer in the development of pastoral counseling. I never regretted the move and found Dr. Wise to be a fine scholar and the pioneer he was purported to be. I studied at Garrett for two

13

years and received my Master of Divinity degree. As thorough as I consider Carol Wise and others to be, I do not recall a single discussion, in class or out, of the homosexual phenomenon.

I credit Wheaton College, Northern Baptist Seminary, and Garrett Seminary for teaching me to think and research. They all taught me to do good research and to have confidence in my research. However, specifically on the subject of homosexuality, they left me totally unprepared for the pastoral task that lay ahead of me in relating to homosexuals. I have seen no indication that Christian colleges and seminaries are doing any better by their present crop of students.

I am an American Baptist who is somewhat conservative. I suspect this book will be labeled by some as "liberal." I do not see it in that light. American Baptists have faced this dilemma often. We consider ourselves biblical people with a social conscience. In some settings, it makes us appear liberal. This is my dilemma in dealing with the subject of homosexuality. I see my conclusions and convictions flowing out of commitment to biblical faith. My hope and plea is that those who read this book will set aside liberal and conservative bias and simply hear the story and listen to the issues that are presented. Christians of all shades and varieties must sort out the facts and discard the untruths if we are to find answers to the relationship of churches and homosexuals.

The organization of this book is important to its argument. Section One is autobiographical. It is the story of my own step-by-step experience of being pastor to gay and lesbian persons. The experience itself forced me into research and study on a subject I would have been more comfortable ignoring. In retrospect I admit with a little shame that I have never gone out of my way to be a pastor to gay and lesbian persons. Once word was out that I was willing to be their pastor, they have sought me out in a continuing stream. With every new pastoral experience I have been forced to read more, study more, think more. A fuller understanding of the homosexual population can come only as non-homosexual persons decide to be open to friendships with persons with a sexual orientation different from their own.

It is my hope that the reading of this book will be encouragement to the reader to begin such a journey. If one makes such a journey, it will be life changing. Deciding to build bridges to gay and lesbian persons is frightening because it is a world of the unknown to the heterosexual person. I have always loved biography. Taking a journey with someone else has been encouragement to take one of my own. I am asking you to accompany me on my journey in the hope that you will decide to take your own.

Section II is my own modest proposal for churches. It begins with a review of what has happened in the past twenty-five years. Churches and church leaders need to be familiar with key events and key writings to grasp the task that lies before us.

Next I have written about gay and lesbian persons whom I know, and about whom I am still learning. If we are to make progress, we must know gay and lesbian persons as individuals, not as a category. The material has been read and critiqued by gay and lesbian friends. They have been very helpful. I believe the descriptions are fair and accurate, but at best are incomplete.

As we non-gay, non-lesbian persons begin our learning journey, we find that the gay and lesbian population is rich in diversity. They are not all hair dressers, waiters, or female jocks. There is no such thing as "the gay community." There is a great range of gay and lesbian organizations and communities. Gays and lesbians are every bit as diverse as the general population.

We also find there is no such thing as "the gay lifestyle." Just as there is a great diversity of gay and lesbian organizations and communities; so also is there a great diversity of sexual life styles. Some are celibate. Some are promiscuous. Some are sexually faithful in a monogamous and committed relationship. Some are in heterosexual marriages living a sexual façade.

The point is to introduce the reader to this population that has for so long been condemned, ignored, or misunderstood by most everyone and especially Christian churches. It is only as we begin to grasp the gay and lesbian population that we will be able to turn to the challenge of incorporating believing homosexual persons into the life of churches.

Just how are we to incorporate homosexuals into the life of our churches? It is not enough to say "Welcome." As we face the challenge of the church's ministry to gay and lesbian persons, we must also face their ministry to the churches. They have every bit as much to offer the churches as the churches have to offer them.

I would not claim to have final answers. I do not have a clear picture of what churches would be like if gay and lesbian believers became full partners in our churches. We must together face such pressing issues as ministry to victims of AIDS, sexual ethics and practices of homosexuals, ordination of gay and lesbian ministers, the life of gay and lesbian couples and families in the church, the blessing of sincere couples, and ministry to parents, sons, daughters, brothers, and sisters of gay men and lesbians. What will our churches encourage and advise as more and more gay and lesbian couples want to have and parent their own children? The implications of welcoming gay and lesbian persons into our churches are many.

Where the road leads is unknown, but the beginning of the journey is necessary. We ought not delay any longer. The challenge of the journey is what this book is all about. I have learned that I have no right to reveal who is or is not gay and lesbian. "Coming out" is the challenge and responsibility of each and every person. Once people are "out," I have not felt any necessity to put a cloud over their identity. In the book I have freely changed names and circumstances to protect the identity of people. Even though I have changed names and circumstances, I have always tried to present people as they truly are. In some cases I have felt free to call people by their correct names. I trust I have in all cases been sensitive to the people who are the subjects of this book. I am a very thankful person. Just now I

Introduction

am thankful for every gay and lesbian person who has allowed me the privilege of being a part of their lives. To them I dedicate my book.

Howard H. Bess
Palmer, Alaska
1994

Part I

Personal Journey

Chapter 1

THE FATEFUL CALL

Joe called me and asked for an appointment. I could not have even imagined the journey that was to be launched by that call. I was the pastor of an American Baptist Church in Southern California. I had been pastor of the church for almost ten years. I had been a pastor for fourteen years and felt confident of my pastoral skills. I had learned that ministers were privileged not only to be involved in baptisms, marriages, sermonizing and teaching, but also in funerals, divorces, unwanted pregnancies, heart attacks, alcoholism, and cancer. I believed that the level of trust between the members of the church and me was quite high. Possibly that was the reason that Joe could call me. Possibly it was because he was hurting so badly that he had to talk to someone.

When Joe came into my office, the conversation came right to the point. "Howard, I am a homosexual." I was almost totally ignorant. All I could do was ask questions, assure Joe of my friendship, and make another appointment.

Joe was married. The son whom I assumed to be his turned out to be the son of his wife from a previous marriage. The boy was four years of age and appeared to be very close to his stepfather. The only book that I had ever read on the subject of homosexuality was a book written by psychiatrist Edmond Bergler entitled *Homosexuality, Disease or Way of Life?*[1] It had been a book club selection, and I had received it because I hadn't sent the card saying that I didn't want it. I have a habit of reading books that I buy; and so with a sense of duty, I read it. That was in 1962. Bergler had worked with many homosexuals and had concluded that they were very sick with a treatable disease. I recalled the book and concluded that Joe was sick. I

21

had no idea where to send Joe, so I continued to see him.

Joe certainly had some horror stories to tell. He was very attached to his mother, an alcoholic. His father, now dead, had been a good provider for his family, but he was both a loving father and a tyrant. He struck Joe often and sometimes beat him severely. The father was a truck driver and would be away from his family for several days at a time. Once he had come home and was displeased with something Joe had done and had beaten Joe's bare back with a belt until it was covered with welts and blood. He then consoled Joe by holding him and rocking him throughout the entire night. On another occasion, Joe's father had dug a deep hole in the backyard for some reason. Joe had no recollection of the purpose of the hole; he only recalled that it was very deep—too deep for him to crawl out after his father had put him in the hole as punishment. Joe was left in the hole all night.

As Joe shared more and more of his childhood, I could understand why he would have some sort of mental illness. Joe expressed incredible hostility toward his father and at times wept floods of tears. The more he shared, the more he seemed to remember.

One day as he was walking home from school, a man whom he did not know stopped and offered him a ride. Joe accepted but soon realized that the man was not taking him home. He took him somewhere into some bushes or woods and sexually molested him. When Joe shared this particular incident, he expressed the opinion that this must have been the incident that had turned him into a homosexual. But Joe's greatest emotional trauma was still to be shared.

Joe called me one day in a panic and said he must talk to me immediately. I was free so I invited him to come to my office. I had never seen Joe so emotionally distraught. He could hardly speak. He had remembered something that he wanted to believe had never happened. But he knew that it was true. Once when his mother was drunk—in his words, "She forced me to have

22

intercourse with her." Joe's sense of guilt was beyond measure. He cried and cried. In the name of Christ, I assured Joe of forgiveness and that the same forgiveness that Christ extends to us was to be extended to his mother as well.

In a certain sense I was pleased with my relationship with Joe. He obviously had trusted me with more of himself than he had ever shared with any other human being. I had been accepting of his anger, and his tears had been understood. A lot of soul cleansing had taken place. I had assured him of God's love and Christ's grace. I also recognized that he needed more help than I could give him, but I did not know where to send him.

It was at that point, so to speak, that the other shoe was dropped. His wife called me for an appointment. I thought I had heard the whole story. Not so. Joe's wife had evidence that he had been sexually molesting her son. When confronted, Joe admitted the molesting. His wife filed for divorce and filed criminal charges against her husband. He was convicted and sent to prison.

While all of these events were taking place, I had decided that I should learn more about homosexuality. I went to the local library and took a look at what was on the shelf. I also read all that was available through the county library system. There was not much. Most of the books by professional therapists took a similar point of view. Homosexuals were sick. Their sickness was treatable if the subject was willing to work at the task of therapy. Such opinions were compatible with my experience with Joe. I believed Joe was sick but that he could be helped with proper treatment.

But then the American Psychiatric Association threw me a curve. In 1973, the APA voted to remove homosexuality from its official list of mental illnesses. They said, "Homosexuality per se implies no impairment in judgment, stability, reliability, or general social or vocational capabilities." The APA said that by the standards of their profession it was unfair to diagnose homosexuals as being psychologically maladjusted if 1) they were not bothering others and were staying out of trouble with the law, 2) they were capable of earning an independent living, and 3) they were capable of forming meaningful relationships with other people. One of the books I found on the library shelf was Troy Perry's autobiographical *The Lord Is My Shepherd, and He Knows I'm Gay.*[2] It was fascinating reading. An ordained Christian minister who had been rejected by his denomination because of his sexual orientation, he had founded the denomination that is now called The Universal Fellowship of Metropolitan Community Churches. Perry did not sound sick to me. He sounded like a sensitive man who had been battered by his denomination.

Then there was the challenge of the Bible passages that deal with homosexuality. I was entirely ill-equipped to deal with the intricacies of the task. Fortunately some Christians were starting to take a closer look at the nine or ten pertinent passages. Dr. Ralph Blair was one of those pioneers. Blair, a clinical psychologist, was the President of the Board of Trustees of Evangelicals Concerned. He had written a booklet on the subject.[3] It made sense to me and was encouraging.

I felt that I had to have a working understanding, even if it were tentative. My tentative conclusions were 1) homosexuals are attracted to partners of the same sex because of some flaw in early childhood rearing or psychological trauma; 2) homosexuals never choose their sexual orientations but are responsible for choosing specific homosexual actions; 3) homosexuality is treatable, but the time and costs are prohibitive for most; 4) homosexuals should be received into the full life of the church just as all the rest of us sinners have been received.

Joe was sent to a prison for the criminally insane. There he was given therapy with the assumption that he was sick and treatable. Joe was a very private person by nature. The treatment was aggressive and he was not always cooperative. I visited him regularly. I made sure that I never became involved in his therapy but maintained my pastoral role. Joe was eventually released and placed on parole. I kept in touch with him, but he seldom came to worship services or other church functions. Because of a parole violation, Joe was sent back to prison. He became very active in the prison chapel and experienced some sort of new spiritual conversion. He was quite enthusiastic about the chapel.

Eventually, Joe was released. He never returned to the church that I pastored. He concluded that the church and I were too liberal. He joined another church. In a few months he was made Scout Master for the church's Boy Scout troop. I lost contact with Joe.

Was Joe a homosexual? In all probability, but one who was seriously mentally ill. Clinically speaking, he was a pedophile. But his pedophilia probably had no more to do with his homosexuality than incest has to do with heterosexuality. I say that Joe was a homosexual because that was Joe's conclusion. His homosexual orientation did not lead to his child molesting. His pedophilia did. These are conclusions that I reached after relating to Joe over the years. While in the midst of relating to Joe, I was at times thoroughly confused. It has been only after years of reading, studying, and involvement with homosexual persons that I have some coherent understanding of him.

The phone call from Joe was one of those key incidents that end up having significance beyond anyone's imagination. It is an example of what the pastoring responsibility is all about. Someone in need comes and says, "Help me." Pastors, as inadequate as we may feel, have no right to refuse. The ministry of God's grace and mercy has been placed in our hands. I never for a moment felt that I could refuse to be Joe's pastor. The fact that I was ignorant and ill-prepared had nothing to do with my responsibility to respond as best I could as a pastor.

But I had no right to remain ignorant. As I began to learn about gay and lesbian persons, I also began to realize how many of them there are. I also learned how badly Christian churches have treated and are treating them. Our churches have committed unconscionable sins against homosexuals, and pastors have perpetuated the sins of neglect. Joe's phone call started the process of my deliverance from further participation in one of the church's ugliest sins and one of the clergy's worst neglects. I am thankful that he called me.

Chapter 2

THE PAPER

Graduate school taught me to be a researcher. Graduate school was a seemingly endless task of reading and writing papers and being forced to reach my own conclusions. When I graduated from seminary, I thought I had found some relief from the research routine. I was very wrong. The preparation of every sermon became a sort of research project. Additionally, I found that I had not learned in seminary all that I needed to know to be the pastor of a church. In seminary other students were readily available with whom I could discuss a variety of topics, and most professors made themselves available as well. Out in the pastorate, I found myself very much alone. When I hit a problem, research was my most available tool.

In addition to sermons, I had written several papers on a variety of subjects relating to the pastoral ministry. They were papers that made no claim to outstanding scholarship, but they were a very good tool that helped me sort out my own thinking. When I was faced with the new challenge of ministry to homosexuals, it was only natural that I decided to write a paper.

My experience with Joe was just a starter. My ignorance drove me to the public library. The more I read, the more aware of the homosexual population I became. My contact with gay and lesbian persons expanded. The more contact I had with homosexuals, the more closely I looked at the Bible passages that seemed to say something on the subject. I talked with my ministerial colleagues on the subject. Most did not even want to talk about the subject. Some were extremely condemning of homosexuals. Almost all were ignorant and had little motivation to be otherwise. Even though I was in the early phase of my learning, I found that I knew more about the subject than any

27

other clergyperson I could find.

The Paper was a modest effort, about 16 pages in length. It carried a bibliography of books by psychiatrists, psychologists, and sociologists but only four books written from a Christian perspective. I made sure the readers of *The Paper* knew that my conclusions were tentative. My understandings expressed in *The Paper* were 1) the phenomenon is rooted in early childhood development, 2) a person's sexual orientation is never chosen, 3) the phenomenon is treatable, and 4) with grace the church was to accept homosexuals as brothers and sisters in Christ.

Having written *The Paper,* what further use was to be made of it? I called a Sunday evening meeting of the congregation, presented *The Paper*, and asked for comments. I had no idea what would happen. I was surprised at the cautious but positive response.

As a direct result of the open handling of the subject, I discovered several closeted gay and lesbian persons in the congregation. I discovered that gay and lesbian persons have parents, sisters and brothers, and children. I discovered that the whole subject was one that people wanted to discuss in general but one that people did not want to discuss in the particulars of their own relationships and experiences.

Several people were helpful to me and the congregation. One was a retired American Baptist educator. Following their retirement, he and his wife had settled in our area and joined the church. He was highly regarded in the church. The evening when *The Paper* was presented, he spoke up with his counsel: We had much to learn, and we should learn all we could. To those who were disturbed by *The Paper,* he urged caution and tolerance. I was always thankful for this gentleman. Although he did not necessarily agree with me, he asked people to listen. He probably saved me a lot of grief. I encourage all pastors to develop a thought-out approach to homosexual people in the ministry of the church. I would not necessarily think pastors should call a congregational meeting cold turkey and share what they know. A pastorate could be significantly shortened. On the other hand, I believe there is considerable wisdom and willingness to listen in every congregation. Pastors are probably not nearly as alone as they might at times think.

The Paper was helpful to me in my pastoral ministry. I made dozens of copies of *The Paper* and they were always there for interested people. Gay and lesbian persons welcomed *The Paper* because they then knew how they stood with the church and its pastor. It was used by gay and lesbian persons to "come out" to their parents and friends. Occasionally other clergy persons would use a copy to help people in their own congregations.

The challenge of understanding homosexual people did not end with the writing of that first paper. It was only a beginning. I bought almost every book I saw on the subject of homosexuality, especially if it related to the Bible, Christianity or the church. I found that with new information and new insights, I had to keep revising *The Paper.* I wish now that I could call back the earliest editions, but since that is not possible, I can only hope people remember my conclusions were labeled as tentative. Even now, my conclusions are tentative. But ministry with homosexual persons cannot wait for final answers.

The Paper in its various editions traveled far and wide. The appearance of *The Paper* in Anchorage, Alaska is a major factor in my pilgrimage of ministry. *The Paper* has been presented to large groups of ministers, distributed in some circles within my own denomination and in ecumenical circles in Anchorage, and significantly, in the Alaska State Prison system.

The Paper has been discussed, rejected, embraced, despised, and praised. All the reactions have contributed to my own learning and deepening convictions. When I received that first phone call from Joe, I had no idea where the phone call would take me. When I first decided to write a paper, putting my best understanding and convictions in black and white, I had no idea what a 16-page paper could do to my career as a minister.

Chapter 3

BLIND ALLEY

Hank, his wife Jean, and their seven-year-old son began attending the church. They were a delightful couple and from all appearances, they were happily married. Their son was a good-looking boy, bright and socially well adjusted. While most pastors welcome people no matter what problems they might have, we like to see some who come with healthy bodies, marriages, and lifestyles. Hank's family fit the image.

Hank was an engineer at one of the local research installations. Jean worked outside the home as an interior decorator. They lived in a comfortable home. Both were especially goodlooking. He was ruggedly handsome and wore a well-trimmed beard. If anyone had suggested that Hank was gay, everyone would have laughed in derision.

I received a phone call from Jean, asking if she could speak with me. We made a luncheon date. Several couples in the church participated in Marriage Encounter. In our area it was a well-established and respected program with religious emphasis that helped couples with good marriages to have even better marriages. Hank and Jean had attended a weekend Marriage Encounter. It had been a total disaster.

During a Marriage Encounter weekend, husband and wife are encouraged to do a lot of very personal sharing. They do so in writing and share with one another what they write. In the process of sharing, Hank revealed to Jean that he was gay. She was devastated. She and Hank had been married for over ten years. While their sexual relations had never operated at a high level of passion, they loved one another and especially enjoyed parenting their son together.

Hank was very open to talking with me as his pastor. He

31

had known that he was gay when he and Jean were married. He married her first of all because he truly liked her, having known her since they were teenagers. He wanted to have a family and knew that his acceptance in society would be much easier in a heterosexual marriage. He even reasoned that under the practice of heterosexual relationships, he might in fact become heterosexual. It didn't work.

In the ten years of marriage, Hank had never once been able to have intercourse with Jean except when he fantasized that she were a man. He found no satisfaction in their sexual relations, always faking it, always feeling guilty about this terrible dishonesty. He had become attracted to another man and had been having an extended affair with him. The sharing at Marriage Encounter brought him to a moment when he could no longer continue the dishonesty involved in the marriage.

Hank would have stayed in the marriage. The paper that I had written stated ". . . the highly motivated homosexual can with skilled help become a thorough heterosexual, emotionally and functionally."[4] I had quoted psychiatrist Daniel Cappon from his 1965 book *Toward An Understanding of Homosexuality*. Cappon made the statement that he wanted, ". . . to leave no doubt that homosexuality is curable. It is, in fact, as curable, remediable, and ameliorable as the patient wishes."[5] Hank wanted to save his marriage. He wanted to be a heterosexual.

Jean was not willing to wait to see if this could happen. She filed for divorce.

A copy of *The Paper* had fallen into the hands of a clinical psychologist in private practice in the community. He was surprised to meet a Baptist minister with these concerns. He contacted me, and we became good friends over the next few years. I had referred parishioners to him for counseling, and they had been well satisfied with his work. We had extended conversations about homosexuality, and he embraced the understanding that was prevalent at that time among counseling professionals. Homosexuality was a treatable illness. He theorized that our sexuality operated from deeply seated images in the brain.   He believed that through intensive psychotherapy the faulty images which produce the homosexual phenomenon could be removed and replaced by opposite sex images that would leave the person thoroughly heterosexual.   He claimed significant success with other homosexual patients.   Hank was a highly motivated client.   I referred him to my clinical psychologist (Ph.D.) friend.

Hank saw the therapist for many months, typically more than once a week.   Therapy was expensive and not covered by insurance.   Hank had been quite generous with his wife in their divorce settlement and was very conscientious in seeing that his son was properly supported.   He had some savings but went through all he had and borrowed money from his family to continue the intensive therapy.   At times Hank thought he might be making progress; but more realistically, he knew that in spite of his efforts, his sexual orientation was as homosexual as ever.

My reaction was one of real surprise.   I could not imagine a more highly motivated subject than Hank.   The work that was being done by the therapist was very much in line with what I had been reading in books by a variety of therapists.   It was a sad day for both of us when Hank shared with me that he was gay and that he was now convinced nothing could change that reality.   I felt bad because I had offered a hope that turned out to be a very expensive blind alley.

Hank continued to be active in the church; we continued to be very good friends.   He is in an apparently successful and satisfying long-term relationship with another man.   He continues to be an excellent father to his son.   He still likes his former wife, and they have a positive relationship.

My experience with Hank sent me back to the drawing boards of my understanding.   Hank seemed so normal to me.   He seemed like a whole person.   He was kind, generous, and loving.   He was masculine by every definition except for his sexual orientation.   He was not sexually promiscuous.   He was socially at ease with both men and women. Some of his closest friendships were with women in the church. I concluded that Hank not only seemed normal, he was. Hank not only seemed like a whole person, he was.

I had sent one of the finest men I have ever known down a blind alley. I revised my thinking and rewrote *The Paper*.

Chapter 4

NEW INSIGHT

The more I related to gay and lesbian persons, the more the challenge of understanding them grew. New insight came when I met Joan and Rose. They appeared as visitors at the regular eleven o'clock Sunday worship service of the church. Both were goodlooking women: Joan, tall and slender; Rose shorter and a little on the pudgy side. They signed the guest register, and as was my custom with all visitors, I paid them a visit at their apartment. After exchanging pleasantries, I asked about their religious background. Joan took a shortcut and said, "Howard, I want you to know that we are lesbians; we have been together for three years, and we are very happy in our relationship."

Most gay and lesbian people that I have known are very cautious about sharing their sexual orientation. Further, they usually show some signs of anxiety when they do share. This was not the case with Joan. It was obvious to me that she was comfortable with her sexuality.

With that subject out of the way, we then proceeded to talk about their relationship to God and the church. Rose had been raised in a very devout American Baptist family in the Midwest. She had always gone to Sunday School. As a teenager she was active in the Baptist Youth Fellowship. She had made a public commitment to Christ as a teenager. Her faith was important to her. She had attended an American Baptist-related college for two years, but then dropped out of college and had not returned.

Joan's experience was quite different. She had a stable family and had grown up with a healthy relationship with both mother and father. The family was not church connected, and God played no big part in her childhood or teen years. Joan was

35

obviously very bright. She had graduated from a state university in the Midwest. She had continued her education and earned a Master's degree in social work, specializing in gerontology. Gerontology was a new and expanding field and finding employment was never a problem for her. Southern California has a very large senior population, and Joan knew she could find a job with ease when she and Rose moved from the Midwest.

Joan had been interested in religion as an intellectual fascination all through her higher education experience, but it became more personal when she and Rose met, dated, and then made long-term commitments to eachother. When they decided to make their move to California, they also decided it was time to sort out their relationship to God and establish a lifestyle that took God seriously. Rose's greatest problem was her relationship with her family. When she had told her parents that she was lesbian, she also told them about her love for Joan and their relationship. The reaction of her parents was all too typical. Rose had been led astray. She was involved in evil. The Bible condemns homosexuals. Don't ever bring Joan around us. She was overjoyed to find an American Baptist church where she and Joan could be open about their relationship and be accepted. She was delighted to have a pastor who did not want to change her sexual orientation. This was my first opportunity to try to fulfill my calling as a minister of reconciliation between a lesbian and her parents. After talking with Rose at length, I wrote her parents a long letter and sent them a copy of *The Paper*. They responded in a letter that I considered positive but cautious. It was obvious that the pastor of their American Baptist church and I did not see things in the same way. The exchange did put Rose and her family back in communication with one another. Eventually I moved to another pastorate, so I do not know the eventual outcome of the relationship between Rose and her family. But a start toward reconciliation had been made.

Joan was an eager learner, and she was determined that her lack of religious background and knowledge would be short-lived. She read voraciously. I was only too happy to feed her Christian reading materials. Joan was a warm person, but she would not allow her heart to go anywhere without her head. When she decided she wanted to follow Christ, it was wholehearted and with no mental reservations. I had the privilege of baptizing Joan, and it was a baptism that I will never forget.

The church had built a sanctuary without a baptistry. Baptistries for Baptists are very expensive pieces of plumbing. We use lots of water. As a cost-saving move, the baptistry had been eliminated. Fortunately we had access to lots of water. Several members of the church had backyard swimming pools. All our baptismal services were held at the home of one or another of our pool-owning members. Chairs were carried in and the congregation ringed the pool. Attendance was especially large for this particular service. The whole neighborhood rang with our singing. Joan, along with two others, was baptized on a Sunday afternoon in May. It was a beautiful sunny day. Joan was an exuberantly happy twenty-eight-year-old woman. I had a strange sense of God's presence that day. Somehow I felt I could hear the voice of God saying, "This person is special."

Joan and Rose remained very active members of the church until I left for another pastorate. But Joan's walk with God was just beginning. Joan felt that God was calling her to become an ordained minister. She was encouraged by the new pastor of the church to pursue theological education at one of our American Baptist seminaries. She took his advice.

In the process of application, Joan visited the campus of the seminary. She was just as up front about her sexual orientation with a seminary official as she had been with me in our first conversation. She was discouraged from following through with her application.

Joan was not deterred. In her inquiries about seminaries, she found a seminary of another denomination that did not discourage her. She enrolled and loved seminary education.

Three years later she graduated with a Master of Divinity degree. She sought and received ordination in the denomination of her seminary. She is now an active clergy person using her knowledge of older people, her skills as a social worker, and her high sense of calling.

Knowing Joan was a special milestone for me. I had begun ministry with homosexual persons with an assumption that they were damaged people, people who had been dealt a bad hand. My experience with Joan taught me a special lesson. She was not damaged. She, by any standard that might be applied, was a very healthy person. She did not shrink back from who she was. On the other hand she could not be classified as a lesbian activist. She was not out picking fights or waving banners. She was a very healthy, happy human being whom God blessed by calling her to be a minister of the gospel. I gained new insights through Joan. It was worth yet another rewrite of *The Paper.*

Chapter 5

A SLIGHT MISUNDERSTANDING

In 1980 my youngest child was about to graduate from high school. I was single and looking forward to a new marriage. It was time to leave Southern California and move on to ministry in another setting. I put my name into the American Baptist personnel system and waited for a phone call or a letter. I received a call from Max Oliphant, one of our American Baptist regional staff in Seattle, Washington. "Howard, would you consider going to Anchorage, Alaska?" I had always told the Lord I would go wherever the Spirit led, but the thought of Alaska had never crossed my mind as a possibility. Further, I did not know Anchorage, Alaska from Fairbanks, Juneau, or Nome. After a good laugh, which Max fully understood, I said, "Sure, why not?"

The phone call was followed by correspondence and phone calls to and from the search committee of an American Baptist Church in Anchorage. I liked the people with whom I spoke, and the needs of the church sounded challenging and interesting. In the process of the communications, the committee asked me to send various materials that reflected my ministry and beliefs. I sent a variety of materials that I had used in my most recent pastorate in California. I included several copies of the church newsletter, sermon tapes, and a short statement of my theological beliefs. While putting together the package of materials, I faced the great question. Should I include a copy of *The Paper*? Believing that I had to be fully honest with the Anchorage congregation, I included a copy. I had "put out the fleece."

The next step in the process was a conference phone call from the full search committee. It lasted an hour. I didn't know what to think. The subject of homosexuality was never mentioned. I was frankly relieved. By that time I was fascinated by the thought of going to Alaska. The church then invited me to Anchorage to meet the congregation. I spent five days in Anchorage. I met the search committee. I met the congregation. I preached at their Sunday worship service. I was hosted royally. The people of the congregation could not have been more gracious. I thought it was strange, however, that the subject of homosexuality was never raised, and I was never asked about my attitude toward gay and lesbian persons. There were times I wanted to raise the subject, but I reasoned that I had done my part in sending *The Paper*.

Two years later I discovered what had happened. The chairperson of the search committee received and opened the package I had sent. She saw *The Paper* and was delighted with it. She had gay and lesbian friends who had suffered significant rejection and discrimination. *The Paper* was a good reason for her to be strongly supportive of my coming to the Anchorage church. She reasoned that others might not share her attitude and felt that I might not be called because of *The Paper*. She withdrew *The Paper* from the materials and no other person from the church saw it.

I was called to be the pastor of the Anchorage church and began pastoring with the assumption that at least the key leadership of the church was aware of my attitudes and commitments. Assumptions are very dangerous as I was later to learn.

My daughter Jill is an actress. She had received her degree in theater from the University of California, Irvine. She then stayed in the Los Angeles area pursuing her career. Los Angeles is a tough market, and she became one of a legion of starving performers. She retreated to Anchorage where she knew she could count on room and board, and she immediately became active in Anchorage theater. While playing a role for Alaska Repertory Theater, she met Tom Wilkinson. Tom had recently gone through a very difficult experience. A devout Episcopalian and gay, he had served the church in various capacities and had been encouraged to pursue seminary training. He had completed his Master of Divinity degree at an Episcopal seminary and returned to Anchorage fully expecting to be ordained. Recommending ordination became difficult for Tom's Anchorage parish because of his sexual orientation. The church refused to make the needed recommendation, and Tom's hopes for ordination died. He was angry and bitter.

Jill was well aware of my attitudes. She had many gay and lesbian friends and felt very comfortable around them. In a conversation with Jill, Tom poured out his agony. She assured him that her father was not homophobic and would not back down from his convictions. Soon Tom had occasion to test me.

C. Wayne Hussey had died. He was the unquestioned leader of the gay population in Anchorage: he was high profile; he had served in high positions in gay organizations; he was respected and cherished by the gay population. Tom Wilkinson along with two other gay leaders, Ed Nicely and Jim Morgan, wanted to lead a memorial service in Hussey's honor. They needed a place in which to hold the service, so Tom called me. My response was, "Yes, we would be honored to host the service."

The church building was packed. The congregation was a who's who of gay organizations and communities. I later learned most were wondering how it happened that such a service was being held in a Baptist church. Suddenly, I was a person known to many gay and lesbian people, and the church I pastored was identified as a place friendly to homosexuals.

Tom, Ed, and Jim were all aspiring ministers. All had been spurned by their churches; and for one reason or another, each had become disenchanted with the Anchorage Metropolitan Community church. They decided to start an independent church with the specific goal of ministering to the Anchorage gay and lesbian population. They pulled together a small group and began looking for a place to meet. Again Tom came to see me.

41

While I had felt free to grant use of the church's facilities for a one-time use without consulting the Board of Deacons, I felt that Deacon Board approval was needed for a regular, every Sunday use. I let Tom know that I was supportive and took the matter to the Deacons.

The Deacon Board found itself operating in strange territory. While they knew they had the authority to say "yes" or "no," they chose not to make the decision and referred the request to the whole congregation. The meeting was well advertised and was the largest congregational business meeting in the history of the church. Members who had not attended any service of the church in years suddenly appeared. The meeting was high with emotion. Voting was by secret ballot. When the vote was counted, the congregation voted by a two-vote margin to disallow the new congregation the use of the church facilities for worship. Reality had set in.

For the short run, the "no" vote probably saved the church. If the vote had been "yes," many people would have left the congregation. The church would have been devastated. But for the long run, the effect was a somewhat uneasy tension that marked the congregation as long as I remained its pastor.

In retrospect, the withholding of *The Paper* was unfortunate. The well-intended action of one person had prevented an open discussion of the issue in an atmosphere that was calm, friendly, and less threatening. At no time during the seven years of my pastorate in Anchorage was there an opportunity for me as pastor to teach, share, and discuss this vital issue. When I left the Anchorage church, no one knew the extent of the work and research that I had done. Neither did they know the extent of my ministry with gay and lesbian persons in Anchorage.

The hosting of the funeral of C. Wayne Hussey and my strong advocacy for the church to rent its facilities to a predominately gay congregation established me as a friend of the gay and lesbian population of Anchorage. They now trusted me and welcomed me into their communities. My wife and I were invited to gay social events; occasionally we participated. I was invited to give the invocation at various gay celebrations such as the Gay Pride Ball. Several gay and lesbian persons made the church I pastored their home church. I was pastor to many who never entered the church door. Gay and lesbian persons who were struggling with spiritual issues were referred to me by professional counselors. I gave away dozens and dozens of copies of *The Paper.*

In this process of being welcomed by gay and lesbian people, I grasped more fully the extent of the homosexual population. Gay bars were packed and social events were well attended; prominent people from the business, professional, and government worlds emerged. Everywhere I looked, I saw people who I knew were gay or lesbian.

The misunderstanding between me and the church eventually led to my leaving. It also ushered me into a richly rewarding relationship with the diverse homosexual population of Anchorage.

Chapter 6

IDENTITY

There are many structures in the homosexual population. Some of it is informal. Some of it is highly organized, and purposes are carefully defined. An organization which is very important to the Alaska homosexual population is Identity, Inc. Identity is a 501(c)(3), federally tax-exempt, non-profit corporation. Its purposes are education, advocacy, and service. When I first became aware of Identity, Jay Brause was Executive Director. Jay is bright, aggressive, and very articulate. While he has never been THE leader of the state's gay and lesbian population, as Executive Director of Identity, he was often the spokesman for them. Jay asked me if I would consider joining the Board of Directors of Identity. I said yes and entered into a whole new phase in my relationship with homosexuals. During the three years I served on the Identity Board, a woman attorney and I were the only non-gay, non-lesbian members.

During the period of my involvement with Identity, I received a new measure of education about homosexuals, who they are, and the nature of their concerns. Four distinct experiences were eye openers. The first was my experience with the lesbian population.

I had some significant contact with lesbians in California, but my experience with homosexuals there had been primarily with gay men. At any given time, about half of the board members of Identity were lesbians. They tended to be bright, talented, aggressive and successful in their vocations. Lesbians in Alaska are effectively organized, both socially and politically. Groups network with one another, from Juneau to Anchorage to Fairbanks. They are less visible than gay groups, but they are more focused and effective in what they do. They remain more closeted from the general population than do their male counterparts.

The typical lesbian that I came to know in significant numbers was living in a committed relationship with another woman. In most cases one or both of them had children from a previous heterosexual marriage. It was from their experience of heterosexual marriage that they concluded they were irrevocably homosexual. They were good parents. They lived well. In the work place they were simply single women sharing living expenses with another single woman. Society places little or no particular stigma on such outward appearances. In fact, they were lesbians who loved one another deeply and who had made lifelong commitments to one another.

Today, the great unknown statistic about homosexuals is the number of lesbians in our midst. Those who are living in same-sex relationships are somewhat hidden from the researchers; even more hidden are the women, lesbian by sexual orientation, who continue to live in sexually sterile heterosexual marriages. They do so to meet society's social expectations. Such women come to organizations like Identity seeking wisdom and answers. Having come to know several in these circumstances, I suspect the lesbian population is as large as the gay population; it is just more hidden to both the general public and to sex researchers.

The next eye opener came from Identity's Helpline operation. A very modest project, Helpline operated only on Friday and Saturday evenings from nine to midnight. The only advertising was a simple three-line ad in the personals section of the classifieds in the local paper; however, the phones rang continuously. About half the calls were crank calls, the other half from desperate and hurting people. The adults who called followed a familiar pattern: they were deeply closeted homosexuals. Typically they had never told another person of their sexual orientation. Many had never had any same-sex sexual experiences, but they knew they were attracted to persons of the same sex and never to the opposite sex. Some were trapped in

46

heterosexual marriages and had no idea what to do. They had no one with whom they could speak. They could not speak to their pastors because typically pastors have either said nothing or have spoken out with unrelenting condemnation. They were church officers, choir members, teachers, engineers, business people, and public employees. One theme ran through all the non-crank calls—fear. The anonymity of Helpline allowed them to speak freely.

One group of callers was especially troubling to me. Of the non-crank calls, fully one-half were from teenagers, almost always boys. Trying to sort out their sexuality, they had concluded that their sexual feelings did not match up with those of the majority of their teenage friends. They felt no sexual attraction to girls. They felt attracted to other boys. They had heard about homosexuality only in derogatory terms. They were confused. They were frightened. They had not been recruited or lured into their dilemma. Typically they had never talked to anyone about these feelings and urges. They were absolutely alone.

Many of these teenagers were very religious. Their religious affiliations covered the full spectrum: Presbyterian, Roman Catholic, Baptist, Lutheran, Assembly of God, Nazarene, Methodist, Pentecostals. The phenomenon was no respecter of denominations. Their religious affiliation made their anxiety worse. Many of their churches were teaching that a homosexual was destined for Hell—no exceptions. Almost everyone is afraid to talk to teenagers who are going through this experience. Gay organizations are very afraid of offering counsel of any kind. In so doing, they open themselves to the charge of recruiting. My name was given to many gay teenagers with religious questions; few called. Only rarely did I talk to a gay teenager face to face. When I did, it was with caution and a bit of fear. I was talking to another pastor's sheep, and in the process, I was criticizing another pastor's beliefs and judgments.

Whenever I am in the halls of a school or around any

group of teenagers, my mind inevitably says "One in ten, one in ten." I believe they are the loneliest of the lonely, and it is believed that they will account for 30 percent of all teenage suicides.

Identity also brought about my pastoral involvement with victims of AIDS. Homosexuals understood the magnitude of the AIDS tragedy before the general public showed any concern. Identity was given a small grant by the Municipality of Anchorage to disseminate information about AIDS and safe sex. Identity became the distribution point for condoms and various brochures. The task was effectively accomplished with efficiency. Gay bars and gay organizations were flooded with materials. Support groups for those who tested HIV positive became readily available.

Those associated with Identity and the AIDS education program knew far more than the Anchorage office of the federal Center for Disease Control. Those involved with Identity always knew more men in Anchorage who tested HIV positive than were being reported by the CDC. Many left the state of Alaska as soon as they tested positive. They left to be near medical centers where they felt treatment was more available. The people involved with Identity saw what lay ahead, and they cared deeply. AIDS was not something we read about in the paper. It was people we knew, and I came to believe I had no choice but to be their pastor.

The fourth Identity activity that had a lasting effect on me was their involvement in research. A study of the gay and lesbian population in Alaska had never been done. Identity decided to conduct such a study. Identity applied for a research grant from the Chicago Resource Foundation and was successful. It also received a small grant from the Municipality of Anchorage. The study was published in 1986, just prior to my joining the Board of Directors. It was entitled *One in Ten.*[6] While such a study of the gay and lesbian population had not done in Alaska, studies had been done in other parts of the country. Identity reviewed a study made in Boston and adopted their model for the Alaska project. There was very good cooperation among gay and lesbian organizations in the distribution of questionnaires across the state. Dozens of volunteers made the survey possible. Melissa Green, a very talented activist for gay and lesbian rights, was the principal organizer and writer of the report. By every standard of sociological research, *One in Ten* was a fine piece of work. The number of respondents was unusually high. From *One in Ten*, my understanding of the gay and lesbian population was made more concrete. Here are some of the statistics that I found especially significant:

- 43% of all respondents had a four-year college degree or higher.

- 41% of all respondents were home owners.

- 21% had served in the armed forces.

- 31% of males had served.

- 25% were, or had been, married to a member of the opposite sex.

- 19% had children.

- Respondents first recognized their homosexual orientation at an average age of 12.5 years.

- After recognizing their homosexual orientation, it was an average of eight years before a respondent told anyone about his/her sexual orientation.

- 71% had experienced some form of discrimination because of their sexual orientation.

- Over one-third recognized they were, at least potentially, problem drinkers.

- Over two-thirds had used drugs other than alcohol.

- 58% no longer identified themselves with any religious tradition.

- 86% were registered voters; and of those, 87% voted regularly.

One in Ten said to me that the gay and lesbian population is far more sinned against than sinner. Its members live in fear and long for acceptance of family, church, and society. It is a troubled population that needs help and especially needs pastors.

The second study conducted by Identity focused on the 71 percent of the *One in Ten* respondents who reported they had experienced some form of discrimination. Identity again turned to the Chicago Resource Center Foundation for funding. Melissa Green continued as the key organizer and writer. She was joined by Jackie Buckley, another very talented activist for gay and lesbian rights. Jay Brause, who had become a full-time sociology student at the University of Alaska Anchorage, was principal researcher on employment and housing discrimination against gay men and lesbians. The same high quality of research that was found in *One in Ten* was also found in *Identity Reports, Sexual Orientation Bias in Alaska*.[7] Here are some of the key findings:

- 31% of Anchorage employers would not hire or promote and would fire someone

they   had   reason   to   believe   was
homosexual.

•   20% of Anchorage landlords would either
       not rent to or would evict someone they
       had reason to believe was homosexual.

Buckley and Green interviewed gay and lesbian persons
and gathered 84 signed statements about actual incidents of bias,
discrimination, harassment, or violence in Alaska.   *Identity
Reports,* published in 1989, leaves little doubt about the reality of
discrimination against homosexuals.   I am left bewildered that
churches, who have a strong tradition of justice, look the other
way as though nothing is happening to such a significant segment
of society.

Chapter 7

AIDS

Today the churches' ministry with homosexuals cannot be separated from ministry to people dying of illnesses related to AIDS. My first involvement with someone dying of an AIDS-related illness came at the request of a gay friend. He had a friend who was going through his final illness. His friend was an Alaska Eskimo and was hospitalized at the Alaska Native Hospital. His religion was fundamentalist Christian, and he had been told AIDS was God's judgment on him for his homosexuality. His family had turned their backs on him. He was alone except for a small circle of Anchorage gay men. I visited him twice before he died.

I found that I had nothing to say to him that I would not have said to any person in the throes of dying. God loved him and, in Christ, had provided for his eternal life. We have all sinned, but God in Christ has decided to deal with us according to His grace, rather than our sins. By trusting the work of Christ on the cross, we can pass from this world with peace and confidence. I held his hand; I embraced him each time I left. I had no fear of the particular medical travesty that was taking his life. My belief system and training and experience as a pastor did not allow me to see him as different from any other dying person. The gospel was still good news and had its same redeeming power.

My young Eskimo friend, whom I knew so briefly, was the first of many. I have pastored others who lingered with the realities of AIDS for years before death claimed them. I have always struggled in pastoring people who are dying. Every dying person reminds me of my own mortality. But I felt no special challenge pastoring people with AIDS. I watched my fellow clergy wring their hands over the challenge of ministering to people with AIDS and could not understand the big deal. Then it dawned on me that my ministerial colleagues were not troubled with AIDS, but with homophobia.

Two examples illustrate the point: Jonathan and his wife were two of the founding members of the small congregation I now pastor in the Matanuska Valley in Southcentral Alaska. Jonathan was a seminary graduate and a hemophiliac. After pastoring a church in Maryland, he decided his health problems and pastoring did not go well together. His wife's family was in Alaska, so Jonathan moved his family to Alaska where he found employment as a social worker. He required a lot of blood products to control internal bleeding and contracted the AIDS virus from a contaminated transfusion. He remained in Alaska until recurring rounds of pneumonia left him unable to work. He and his wife decided to take their three small children and move back to North Carolina near Jonathan's family. They immediately became very active in a Southern Baptist Church in a rural community. Until Jonathan died, their lives revolved around the church fellowship.

During their time in North Carolina they kept close contact with members of the church in Alaska. Their experience with their church in North Carolina was marvelous. Pastor and congregation obviously knew how to minister and support someone who was dying. They did not need any special instructions. Jonathan's AIDS made no difference to his church. But Jonathan was not a homosexual.

George was a very active member of the church I last pastored in California. He and his wife were pillars of the church. George served many years on the church's Deacon Board, and when I left in 1980, he had served three terms as Chairman of the Board. George was an engineer by profession and had a fine career with an electronics research firm. He had a heart attack; by-pass surgery followed. At the time of the surgery he received bad blood, and contracted HIV. The pastors

54

and people of his church knew exactly what to do. The pastors pastored, and the people supported and loved. George died in the loving embrace of an understanding and compassionate church. But George was not homosexual.

How different was the experience of Cliff! Cliff was homosexual and the son of a very prominent American Baptist minister. He had attended one of our American Baptist-related colleges. Rejected by family, he ran away as far as he could. He came to Alaska. He loved Alaska.

While feeling terribly rejected by churches, Cliff never for a minute deserted his faith in Christ. He made his living as a retail sales person, but his loves were photography, traveling, weaving, and music. His Alaska wildlife photography was some of the finest I have ever seen. But he never ever attempted to sell a picture. His values were not of this world. He bought raw wool, spun it into yarn, then knitted sweaters and wove tapestries. He never sold any of his work. He gave it away.

Through a friend he learned that I was accepting of homosexual persons in the church. He called me; we had lunch and talked for long hours. He began attending the church and ultimately joined the membership. Cliff had a fine baritone voice and anchored the bass section of the choir. He played the guitar and blessed everyone with solos and duets accompanied by his playing. He was an excellent cook and blessed church potlucks with great dishes. Everyone was eager to see what Cliff had made on each occasion.

Cliff was in a long-term, monogamous relationship. His partner attended worship services with him from time to time. Cliff had had major surgery and received blood transfusions. Whether he contracted the AIDS virus from bad blood or through sexual contact was never determined. When he learned that he tested HIV positive, he and his partner took one more trip: bicycling through New Zealand. He returned to Alaska and his deterioration became very rapid. He decided he wanted to die in Alaska.

PART I Personal Journey

During the last few months of Cliff's life, I was no longer the pastor of the church. Gay men and lesbians no longer felt welcomed. Cliff and I kept in touch with one another, but during his illness and dying, no one from the church of his membership contacted him. His memorial service was held on the lawn of the home of a former employer overlooking Cook Inlet. Over a hundred people attended. Only five from his church were there.

The three situations with people I dearly loved told me a lot. A Southern Baptist Church in North Carolina knew how to minister to the needs of someone dying of AIDS. But he had a wife and three children. An American Baptist Church in Southern California knew how to minister to the needs of someone dying of AIDS. But he had a wife, children, and grandchildren. An American Baptist Church in Alaska was totally inept in ministering to the needs of Cliff. But Cliff had a lover and was homosexual.

My own denomination produced a packet about ministry to people with AIDS. Conferences were held on the subject. The great shortcoming of the packets and conferences is that the issue of ministry with homosexuals is never faced. My own conclusion is that ministry with people with AIDS is no different from ministry with people dying with cancer, diabetes, or heart failure—unless that person is homosexual.

I continue to lose my friends to AIDS. Even while writing this chapter, I received word that one of my friends had died in Washington state. He had moved from Alaska to be near more sophisticated medical help and to be of help to his partner who had deteriorated more rapidly than he. His partner had been raised as an American Baptist in Upstate New York and he as an independent evangelical in the Chicago area. They both loved God dearly, but the people of God were not so sure God's love should be returned.

Chapter 8

EARLY RETIREMENT

My involvement with homosexuals was a growing source of strain between me and some members of the Anchorage church. A growing number of gay men and lesbians joined the church and even more attended worship services. John and Cliff sang in the choir. Sam played the organ. Gene ushered. When Marie joined the membership, she spoke to the Deacon Board with great warmth about her joy in being accepted into the fellowship of the church with her full disclosure that she was lesbian. Several attended the church who were known to be gay or lesbian only by me. The last Sunday I preached at the church, I recognized that at least 20 percent of the congregation was known to me as being homosexual.

Some of the heterosexual membership had been very supportive but began to be more uneasy as the implications of accepting gays and lesbians became more plain. For those who had read *The Paper*, some things should not have been a surprise. In the edition of *The Paper* that I was then circulating, I plainly stated that "Coupled persons who are homosexual should be respected and blessed." After counsel, and being satisfied with the seriousness of their commitments, I had no hesitancy in blessing gay and lesbian unions. The typical service was very simple, and the guests were few in number.

Early in my ministry at the Anchorage church, I urged the congregation to create a chapel that could be a place of simple spiritual refuge and an intimate place for a variety of small services. Through the generosity of several members and the labor of several others, a chapel was created near the entrance of the church facility. One of the substantial gifts toward the chapel project was from a gay man. I insisted that the chapel be left open 24 hours a day. I know that it became a late night spiritual refuge for him. He has since died of AIDS. It became a place for small gay and lesbian services of union.

One service at which I officiated brought more notoriety than comfort could accommodate. For five years I had been giving a generous amount of time to the volunteer chaplains' ministry in the State of Alaska prison system. I had been assigned to the Meadow Creek-Highland Mountain Correctional Facility at Eagle River. It is a unique facility because both men and women are housed there, and many programs are co-ed. While many of the volunteers carried on programs of personal witnessing, salvation preaching, and directed Bible studies, I brought a different kind of ministry. Over the years, I had become very involved in leading Yokefellow groups, a la Cecil Osborne of Burlingame, California. I brought Yokefellow groups to the state prison system. Yokefellows is an excellent tool by which spiritual concerns can be pursued, and participants can set the agenda. The response was excellent. I do not recall how or when the subject of homosexuality first emerged, but it did. I furnished copies of *The Paper* to anyone who was interested. *The Paper* was soon widely read at Meadow Creek-Highland Mountain. One staff counselor was especially pleased with *The Paper* and sought me out to commend me for it. Gay men and lesbians found their way to my Yokefellow group.

Barbara and Nancy sought me out and asked for a personal visit. They were lesbian lovers who had made long-term commitments to one another. They wanted the blessing of God on their relationship. I had three counseling sessions with them and set the date for a simple service.

In working with gay and lesbian couples, I have never used the word "marriage." I am fully aware that gay and lesbian relationships are not recognized by the state. Neither are they regulated by the state. There were no rules in the Alaska State prison system that prevented me from laying on hands and blessing the commitments of Barbara and Nancy to God and each other.

I reserved a small counseling room at the prison in which to conduct the service. At the appointed hour, I met Barbara and Nancy and two of their friends and held a simple service celebrating their commitments. I drove back to my office. Within fifteen minutes of my arrival at my office, I received a phone call from a reporter from one of the local radio stations. He said he had heard that I had performed a wedding for two lesbians at the Eagle River prison. I told him that I had read a service, laid on hands, and had prayed with two lesbians, but that I had never used the words wedding or marriage. I further told him that I did not think he had a story.

Word spread of the service and came to the attention of the superintendent. He in turn called the coordinator of chaplaincy services for the prison system. I received a call from the coordinator asking me to go with him to talk to the superintendent. I was happy to do so.

The superintendent was very upset with me and told me and the coordinator that I was no longer welcome at Meadow Creek-Highland Mountain. The state immediately transferred Barbara to an Anchorage prison and then to a federal penitentiary in California. As far as I know, Nancy and Barbara have not seen one another since. My gay and lesbian friends around Anchorage were enraged. Two attorneys offered to pursue the incident as a denial of Barbara's, Nancy's, and my civil rights. I indicated I was not interested in such action and it was not pursued.

The chaplaincy coordinator, who had always expressed appreciation for my work and had used me as a trainer for other chaplains around the state, was in a dilemma. Where could he use me? In my own defense, I pointed out that I had earlier given him a copy of *The Paper* about homosexuality and the church, and that it plainly said that as a minister I would do exactly what I had done. He admitted that he had not read *The Paper*. I solved his dilemma and handed him my credentials as an

PART I Personal Journey

Alaska State Prison Chaplain.

People in the church became aware that I was no longer involved in the prison chaplaincy, and I never hid the reasons.

As I had become more involved with the gay and lesbian population of Anchorage, I became more and more aware of the cruelties and discrimination that were heaped on homosexuals day after day. I started looking for more ways in which I could stand with this maligned minority.

One of the major events sponsored by Identity and other groups was the Gay Pride Parade in celebration of the Stonewall* incident. I had earlier either excused myself or was out of town when this event was held. I could no longer keep my identification with them in the shadows. I marched. I was greeted along the entire parade route by my Christian brothers and sisters with their signs of condemnation. I became very glad that I was marching rather than holding signs of condemnation on the curbs of the parade route. The first year my wife, Darlene, declined to accompany me. The next year, she joined me as did my daughter Jill. Word of our participation got back to members of the church's deacon board.

It is hard to tell which straw was the "last straw," but I suspect I know because it was brought to my attention with considerable emotion.

One of my gay friends called me about a friend of his. Richard was starting into physical decline as a result of AIDS-related pneumonia. He was without family in Alaska. A floral designer, but too weak to continue working, he had begun drinking heavily and had lost his apartment for non-payment of rent. He was on the streets. My friend arranged a meeting with Richard.

The Anchorage church has a guest apartment in the

---

*See Part II, Chapter 1, page 69 for an account of the Stonewall Inn resistance.

church complex. It is adjacent to the parsonage which is also in the church complex. Primary use of the guest apartment was the hosting of church officials and missionaries of our denomination. In addition I had been allowed the liberty of giving others shelter as need arose. I had hosted several friends for short periods of time following their release from prison. While there were people in the church who were uncomfortable with the practice, I was never censured or forbidden to make such use of the apartment. I felt free to offer Richard temporary shelter with the understanding that there would be no drinking. He agreed and moved in. The first Sunday of his stay, Richard attended worship service. He was obviously not well. People asked him about his circumstance, and he told them he was living in the church's guest apartment. Some felt that I had gone a step too far.

From 1980, when I began my pastorate in Anchorage, the church grew gradually but not dramatically. Then came an economic downturn which began in 1986. People stopped moving to Anchorage, and there was a dramatic outflow. Before the downturn stopped, 40,000 had left Anchorage. The church lost its share of members. The budget became tighter. I was aware that there were some who left the church because of the homosexual issue. It was in that context that the Deacon Board met in the spring of 1987.

The budget crunch was discussed. I offered to take a substantial cut in pay. The board did not think that was an acceptable solution. Eventually the meeting came to the heart of their concern. Specifically I was asked to lower my profile in my relationship with the gay and lesbian population. I considered every member of the board a friend. I felt no animosity from any member toward me as a person. Any kind of vote that evening would have split the Deacon Board. I felt that would have been injurious to the Church. Further, I had made an earlier promise to myself that I would never be party to a church split.

I took a clean sheet of paper from my notebook and wrote a one sentence resignation. The meeting was concluded.

We embraced one another, and not a few tears were shed. I went home and shared with my wife, Darlene, what had happened. More tears were shed.

At the time of my resignation I was fifty-nine years old. My intention had been to remain active as a pastor until I was seventy. My health was excellent, and I had a good level of energy. I had not lost my zest for life. I felt that I had a good ministerial record. Relocating to another pastorate seemed a reasonable expectation. I activated my personnel file with the American Baptist Personnel Service. I updated the information in the file. In the space provided for Special Areas of Ministry, I wrote "ministry with homosexuals." The director of American Baptist Ministries in Alaska is the denominational administrator to whom I relate most directly. He saw the notation and suggested I delete the entry. He advised that such an entry would probably make me unemployable as an American Baptist minister. I decided that I could not in good conscience take out the notation. He was correct. I never received a single inquiry.

For two years I worked part time as the executive officer of an ecumenical housing ministry. When I turned sixty-two, I retired and began drawing my Social Security and denominational retirement benefits.

Chapter 9

PEACE IN THE VALLEY

The Matanuska Valley is located about forty miles northeast of Anchorage. The Valley was settled in the mid-1930's under one of President Franklin Roosevelt's New Deal depression recovery programs. Over 300 farm families were recruited from the upper midwestern states, relocated in the Valley and given homesteads on which to establish farms. These hardy families carved a farm community out of the Alaska wilderness which is today the primary agricultural center of the state. Two communities, Palmer and Wasilla, about 11 miles apart, anchor the population. Today, besides the farm industry, the Valley serves as a country-style bedroom community for Anchorage.

During my pastorate in Anchorage and under the sponsorship of the Anchorage church and the American Baptist churches of Alaska, a new congregation was planted in the Valley. Three American Baptist families formed the nucleus of the new church. All of the families were personal friends of mine. All three of the men were graduates of Baptist seminaries. Among them they furnished their own pastoral leadership. One was a graduate of Golden Gate Baptist Seminary in San Francisco. He had had a generous exposure to the homosexual population of that area and had come to many of the same conclusions I had. Under the leadership of these three, Church of the Covenant had become a very accepting congregation. There is a high level of tolerance for differing opinions.

When I could not find placement following my resignation from the Anchorage church, Church of the Covenant invited me to be their pastor. They could afford no more than some of my expenses. It was a good match—a small new church that could not afford to pay a minister and a minister who did not need to

63

collect a salary.

Pastoring Church of the Covenant is a part-time responsibility that leaves me with a good bit of discretionary time. I have time to garden, play golf, and watch the Mat-Su Miners play baseball. I serve on the Board of Directors of Daybreak Apartments, a program of supportive living for adults who are chronically mentally ill. I also serve on the board of Mat-Su United Way and give heavily of my time during its fall fund-raising campaign. But the avocation that I enjoy most is writing a weekly opinion column for the local paper, *The Frontiersman*.

Jesus was very much a part of this world, yet he seemed to see it from a unique perspective. My ideal for living is to try to see the world with the mind and eyes of Christ. That was my idea when I approached the publisher of *The Frontiersman* with my proposal for a column written about current events from a religious point of view. I wrote four sample columns for her to read. She liked the material and I have now cranked out a column a week for the past six years. When she left to take another position, I thought my services might be less welcome, but the new publisher was enthusiastic about keeping the column.

"My View" has become a very popular column and regularly draws more letters to the editor than any similar column the editor has ever seen. I write about politics, medical ethics, sex, Desert Storm, Jim Bakker, school funding, patriotism, American foreign policy, and anything else that catches the public concern.

And there is the subject of homosexuality: it is the subject about which no one wants to talk, but about which everyone does talk. If about 10 percent of the population is homosexual, I figure the subject deserves some sort of regular attention. The subject is in the newspapers and other news media often enough that I do not have to go looking for provocation for a column.

Some of the response is predictable. Some church folk flood the paper with letters of outrage. They make generous quotes from the Bible which are consistently irrelevant to the subject. The tone of their letters is hateful and condemning. They repeat untruths about the phenomenon almost always in the name of Christ. Letters of appreciation and support are also received but not in the same numbers as the critical letters.

However, the most significant response is known only to me. Occasionally I receive a negative phone call, but usually the phone calls are calls of appreciation. They are from closeted gays and lesbians, from the parents of homosexuals, and the pastors of churches who agree with me, but who do not dare speak their convictions openly.

We usually think of the social issues surrounding homosexuals as big city concerns. It is true that many homosexuals move to cities because it facilitates openness in some circles while maintaining anonymity toward family and employers. What I have found in the valley is that there is a sizable homosexual population in this out-of-the-way rural setting. I know of no homosexual organizations. The only advocacy group of which I am aware is the chapter of P-FLAG (Parents and Friends of Lesbians and Gays) sponsored by our congregation. Our valley is a good place for gays and lesbians to hide, and hide they do. It will be a few more decades before a gay pride parade will be held in Palmer, Alaska.

In many respects Darlene and I could not be more at peace than we are here in the Matanuska Valley. I love pastoring Church of the Covenant, but I could leave that responsibility with little anguish. I could resign from the boards of Daybreak and the United Way and feel that my life is good and full. I could put aside my typewriter and not write another column for *The Frontiersman* and feel that I have completed my task. However, knowing that there are many hundreds of gay and lesbian young people and adults here who are bewildered, frightened, hiding, and publicly condemned, I cannot abandon them and have peace in my soul, even in the Matanuska Valley. If God gives me twenty or thirty more years of life, my commitment is to use them to bring understanding and justice to our gay and lesbian brothers and sisters. I could not die in peace if I abandoned them in their struggle.

PART II

HOMOSEXUALS, THE CHURCH AND MINISTRY

Chapter 1

THE HOMOSEXUAL PHENOMENON BECOMES OPEN

Events of the past twenty-five years have forced us to acknowledge the presence of homosexuals around us. We have known about their presence, but that truth has been easy to ignore. As I grew up in a small farm town in central Illinois, I was aware of certain rumors. One of the local merchants was supposed to be "funny." The organist at the Presbyterian Church was reported to wear women's panties. When one of the young men of the town was sent home after two years at West Point, the rumor was around that he was dismissed because he liked other boys. But "homosexual" was not in our vocabulary. Other than the kind of reports that circulated around town, I was a thirty-year-old Baptist minister with college and seminary degrees before I was aware of serious discussions of the subject.

A key incident took place in 1969 in New York City. New York City police had raided a gay bar called the Stonewall Inn. Gay men resisted the police, and gay activism was born in the United States. While there were gay bars and gay organizations in every major American city, they had been kept inconspicuous if not hidden. The Stonewall Inn resisters gave courage to gay men all over the country. The annual Gay Pride Day celebrations mark the Stonewall incident. American gay pride marches and gay activism of all kinds look to the Stonewall Inn as their birthplace.

Another landmark date was 1973. In that year the American Psychiatric Association voted to remove homosexuality from its list of mental illnesses. Their reasoning came from the standards of their profession. If homosexuals can hold down regular jobs, establish stable relationships with other people, without bothering others, there is no reason to identify them as being mentally or emotionally ill. Being told that they could be homosexual and emotionally healthy was an enormous boost to the homosexual population.

During this same period of time, television talk shows became a part of the American pastime. The Phil Donahue show was the first of these shows to take full advantage of the public's thirst to examine the details of American life. Donahue and others who copied the format looked for new areas of public discussion. Homosexuality became a hot topic. By this time there was no shortage of available guests for such shows. Gay men started coming out of the closet and into the public eye from every profession and walk of life. The flood gates were open.

What was happening on the American secular scene was accompanied by matching activity in American churches. Until these events began taking place, churches generally looked upon homosexuality as "bad," but they never talked about it. More than any other person, The Rev. Troy Perry forced the issue. Troy was a Pentecostal minister who struggled with his sexual orientation. When he finally accepted and revealed his homosexual orientation, his church rejected him. In Los Angeles in 1968, Troy Perry started the first Metropolitan Community Church. He firmly believed the MCC was a temporary organization that would minister to the gay and lesbian population until denominations of all kinds would rethink their attitude toward homosexuals and welcome them openly into their fellowships. From the humble beginnings in Los Angeles in 1968, the Universal Fellowship of Metropolitan Community Churches has become a major American Christian denomination.

Just as gay activism in America can be dated back to the Stonewall Inn incident in 1969, so the birth of the present upheaval in American churches over the acceptance of homosexuals can be traced to the 1968 birth of the Metropolitan Community Church in Los Angeles.

Gay activism was accompanied by the publication of the first books that forced a rethinking of the homosexual's place in our communities. No book was more significant to the gay and lesbian population than Troy Perry's autobiographical publication entitled *The Lord Is My Shepherd, and He Knows I'm Gay.*[8] It was published in 1972. Four years later Roman Catholic Priest John McNeil wrote *The Church and the Homosexual.*[9] He was a celibate gay priest, who had the scholastic and writing skills to make a first-rate challenge to traditional understandings—biblically, historically, theologically, and psychologically.

Two years later in 1978, Letha Scanzoni and Virginia Ramey Mollenkott published the very provocative *Is the Homosexual My Neighbor?*[10] It was more readable than McNeil's book and was a more popular seller. This book along with McNeil's book became the textbooks, almost the Bibles, for gay and lesbian groups that began springing up in all denominations. Among Roman Catholics the organization was named Dignity. Among American Baptists the name was American Baptists Concerned. Among independent evangelical Christians the organization is Evangelicals Concerned. Similar organizations are flourishing among Lutherans, Methodists, Presbyterians, Episcopalians, and Mormons.[11] A part of the reason these organizations could thrive was that they now had supportive literature produced by writers of standing and integrity.

It was also in 1978 that the massive study of homosexuals was published by the Kinsey Institute. Under the direction of Dr. Alfred Kinsey, the Institute had published the famous "Male" and "Female" reports.[12] The producing of an additional volume on homosexuality had always been a part of Dr. Kinsey's plan. He died before this could be accomplished. The task was revived by Alan Bell and Martin Weinberg of the Institute founded by Dr. Kinsey. The book, simply entitled *Homosexualities,*[13] reports the most massive study of homosexuals ever made. The study inquired about homosexual experiences, the patterns of those experiences, the levels of satisfaction, and the problems. It inquired further into the social adjustments of gays and lesbians, their work, religion, politics, marriages, friendships, and social activities.   As a report of research, it is dull reading.   It is revealing, and within its adopted limits, it is reliable.   No comparable study has been made, before or since.

Early Christian leaders such as Ralph Blair of Evangelicals Concerned tried to take a new look at the Bible and the passages that seemed to be relevant to the homosexual phenomenon, but it was not until 1983 that a more definitive study, *The New Testament and Homosexuality,*[14] was published by Robin Scroggs. Scroggs, New Testament professor at Union Theological Seminary, is a scholar of recognized ability. While his conclusions have been disputed, his basic research has not been challenged. Today, no one can speak seriously to the subject of the New Testament and homosexuality without reference to his work.

More recently William Countryman, New Testament professor at the Church Divinity School of the Pacific (Episcopalian), published another landmark study.[15]   The title, *Dirt, Greed, and Sex*, seems a bit sensational for this careful study of the purity and property codes of the Old Testament, but it is very relevant to the interpretation of passages usually seen as being important to the issue of homosexuality.

It is interesting to note that Countryman and Scroggs do not reach entirely the same conclusions. Further, I am sure that the last word on the Bible and homosexuality has not been written. But with such basic work having been done, the person who wants to come to grips with these topics has been given solid handles.

Notable books on our subject published in the past twenty-five years cannot be discussed without reference to John Boswell's *Christianity, Social Tolerance, and Homosexuality*[16] published in 1980. The subtitle, *Gay People in Western Europe from the Beginning of the Christian Era to the Fourteenth Century* explains the scope and interest of the book. Boswell's work shows that the Christian Church has gone through periods of both tolerance and intolerance toward homosexuals. The patterns of both tolerance and intolerance follow patterns of attitude toward other minority groups; for instance, Jews. Homosexuals were significant contributors to the Christian tradition and ministry when allowed. Boswell in his own stated conclusions warns against anyone setting their conclusions in concrete. The history of the church and its relationship to homosexuals is too unexplored to make definitive statements. The patterns of both acceptance and intolerance are surely there.

More recently Boswell has published another important work. *Same Sex Unions in Premodern Europe*[17] was released in 1994 and further establishes that the Christian Church has at times not just tolerated but openly accepted and blessed same-sex unions.

Another body of literature has developed. It is written and read primarily within the gay and lesbian population. Much of it is highly biographical or autobiographical. Gay and lesbian people are telling their stories of discrimination, defeat, and triumph to one another. Some established publishers have become willing to publish such books, but more important are the new publishers that are uniquely committed to telling the gay-lesbian story. Book stores owned and operated by gays and lesbians that feature gay literature are found in every major American city. Some mainstream bookstores have established sections that feature books of special interest to homosexual customers.

Among gay men and lesbians, *The Advocate* is must reading. *The Advocate*, a biweekly magazine/journal, is a high-quality, slick publication that features both current gay-lesbian news and articles of academic substance.

If a person wants to get acquainted with what is going on in the gay-lesbian world, the newsletters of gay organizations are a windfall of information. I read every word of *The Voice of the Turtle*, the newsletter of American Baptists Concerned. *North View*, the monthly publication of Identity of Anchorage, is a bonanza of information about gay-lesbian activities in the

Anchorage area and a digest of good articles drawn from other publications. *Second Stone* describes itself as "America's Gay and Lesbian Christian News Journal." It is tabloid in form and is a good way to keep up with what is happening to gays and lesbians in the world of churches. The *P-FLAGpole* is another tabloid that is especially helpful with information about legal battles for equality and civil rights.

Today every major Christian body in the United States is scrambling to determine what to do with the strangers in our midst. Twenty-five years ago the same religious groups did not need to address any issue relating to gay and lesbian brothers and sisters because the whole subject was in the closet. Ignoring the issues is no longer possible. The strangers are no longer the strangers they once were. Too many of them have come out into the open. Too much is being written. Information is too readily available. Gay men and lesbians may seem peculiar to people, but no knowledgeable person can deny that they are right beside us, in the same pew.

Chapter 2

WHO ARE THEY?

Accepting that the homosexual phenomenon can no longer be ignored, how are we to understand these recently acknowledged neighbors? The oldest understanding is a religious one. The usual religious verdict has been that homosexuals are evil and same-sex sexual activity is sinful. Homosexuals are to be ostracized and condemned. However, if the homosexual person will repent, God can and will change the homosexual's evil impulses. The gay man or lesbian can be transformed into a functioning heterosexual.

When psychological understanding began challenging religious interpretations, homosexuality was tagged as sickness. Homosexuals were to be treated and transformed into heterosexuals through therapy. Homosexuals in large numbers have gone through counseling without experiencing the projected transformation.

Current popular sociological analysis is more realistic. Homosexuality is seen as a behavioral deviance from a societal norm, but nothing more. If homosexuals are not bothering anyone and are functioning within the law, they are to be at least tolerated and hopefully accepted.

Alfred Kinsey, a sociologist, concluded that homosexuality is not necessarily an either-or proposition. He devised a seven point (0-6) scale.[18] Those who are identified at the 0 end of the scale are considered exclusively heterosexual. Those who are identified at the 6 end of the scale are considered exclusively homosexual. The seven-point Kinsey scale was used in the Kinsey Institute's study of homosexuals and became a self-fulfilling prophecy. The Institute's study leaves the impression that homosexuality is a matter of degree, involves a large part of the total population, and is morally and psychologically neutral.

The Kinsey researchers admitted significant difficulties in getting a large pool of homosexuals to study. The single greatest problem was the homosexual's felt need to remain hidden. To get a pool of participants for their study, the researchers chose the San Francisco area.[19] In retrospect San Francisco was hardly the place to find a normal sampling of the homosexual population. The researchers located their subjects in a variety of ways and places.[20]   Gay bars produced their single largest number of respondents. Their next largest number of participants came from advertising in the print media, primarily newspapers and magazines that target homosexuals.   They also gathered large numbers of participants at gay bath houses and through homophile organizations. I strongly suspect the Kinsey study was significantly compromised by the sources used to recruit respondents.

After working through religious interpretations and after looking long and hard at psychological interpretations, I found myself without a working understanding of homosexuals and homosexuality. After working through the thick volume of the Kinsey Institute study, I found more flaws in the research than I did comprehensive understanding of the homosexual phenomenon.

By the time I read and studied the Kinsey Institute's report I had become acquainted with a significant number of gay men and lesbians.   I could not and still cannot fit the homosexuals I know into the scheme of the Kinsey study. My own experience and knowledge of gay men and lesbians run counter to the descriptions of the Kinsey Institute study.

I cannot claim original research beyond my experiences which are primarily pastoral.   Further, almost all of my involvement has been with homosexual persons who have had strong ties, usually past, with a church, or who have significant spiritual interest. Having recognized that my views are from a somewhat narrow perspective, I submit that they may still be particularly useful to churches and church leaders.

Before answering the question "Who are they?" I believe it is helpful to describe them as I have known them. Following are descriptive statements about the gay men and lesbians I have known and their sexuality:

1) HOMOSEXUALS, EXCEPT FOR THEIR SEXUAL ORIENTATION ARE NOT DIFFERENT FROM THE REST OF THE HUMAN POPULATION. The homosexuals I know are capable of both goodness and evil. They can both create and destroy. They can succeed but also can fail. They can be good parents or inept parents. They treasure companionship and long for intimacy. They can truly love and serve God, and they can tear at the very heart of God. They need Christ's grace and salvation. They are loving. They are angry. They are fearful. All of these statements are true of me and of every heterosexual I have ever known.

2) THE TYPICAL HOMOSEXUAL HAS EXPERIMENTED WITH SEXUAL ACTIVITY AND HAS HAD SIGNIFICANT HETEROSEXUAL EXPERIENCES. Typical homosexuals find their sexuality bewildering. Since they quickly realize their impulses do not meet society's expectations, they experiment with their sexuality, primarily with someone of the opposite sex, not with someone of the same sex.

Gay men and lesbians participate in heterosexual sex for one or more of the following reasons: a) Heterosexuality is the societal norm, and they want to fulfill that norm. b) Heterosexual activity was a part of their sexual experimentation as they sorted out their own sexual identity. c) Opposite sex experiences were a conscious part of their attempt to hide their homosexuality from family, friends, church, employers, and society in general. d) Intercourse with a person of the opposite sex was a part of a concerted effort to change their orientation from homosexual to heterosexual. e) Heterosexual involvement was a part of a deliberate attempt to become a parent.

Many times one or more of these dynamics resulted in the consummation of a heterosexual marriage.

3) HOMOSEXUALS NEVER CHOOSE THEIR SEXUAL ORIENTATION. Given the prejudice and the discrimination homosexuals face, why would anyone make that choice? Homosexual persons find that their sexual orientation is a given. Most gay men and lesbians make valiant efforts to change their sexual orientation to no avail. Sexual orientation can be disciplined but it is never chosen and never changed.

4) HOMOSEXUALS CAN AND DO CHOOSE HOW THEY EXPRESS THEIR SEXUALITY. Heterosexual persons can make either wise or unwise choices about sexual expression. Gay men and lesbians make sexual choices that range from celibacy to promiscuity. In this they are no different than their heterosexual counterparts.

5) BISEXUAL ORIENTATION IS NOT COMMON. By this I am not suggesting that there are no people who are bisexual by orientation. I know a small number of bisexual persons. I make this assertion as a contrary observation to the Kinsey Institute study which found many people in the middle section of Dr. Kinsey's 0-6 scale. I know many people who have had both homosexual and heterosexual experiences. They have had these contrasting experiences for reasons perceived to be valid at the time. I believe many people who have been identified as being bisexual are, in fact, homosexuals who have

sought out both kinds of experiences as they attempted
to sort out the implications of their sexual orientation.

Describing the homosexual person does not answer the
question: "How and why does the phenomenon happen?" Very
few who have spent any time looking at the subject still maintain
sexual orientation comes from a choice.   Freud understood
homosexuality   to   be   developmental.   He   understood
homosexuality in terms of "arrested development," "unresolved
oedipal conflicts," and "irrational phobias." Homosexuality for
Freud was *ipso facto* pathological and was rooted in abnormal
family experience of some kind. This understanding is passe.

In the past some have suggested the phenomenon is the
result of hormonal imbalances.   While hormones can be a
complicating influence on sexual expression, there is no evidence
that hormones are involved in the determination of sexual
orientation as such.

There is mounting evidence that sexual orientation is
inherited and is rooted in genetics. This has not been proven to
a point of universal acceptance. Some will remain skeptical until
the specific gene that determines sexual orientation is identified
and isolated. However, more and more scientists are finding the
evidence already at hand to be overwhelming. Sexual orientation
is as much a product of genetics as are blue eyes and blond hair.

The ultimate conclusion is that homosexual orientation is
a reality that has occurred and will continue to occur in
predictable patterns in the human family. It is a reality that none
of us can escape.

There is a need to define. Definitions help us make
decisions even when we recognize that some definitions are
tentative. A definition of homosexuality must be true to what we
know and the evidence that we have. For a working definition I
offer the following:

*A homosexual is an ordinary person who through no
personal choice finds sexual stimulation and satisfaction from same-*

sex contacts and fantasies which carry no intrinsic religious, psychological, or social impairments.

Chapter 3

WHAT DOES THE BIBLE SAY?

All Christians grant some level of authority to the Old and New Testament writings. When Christians deal with ethics and morality, they either start with the Scriptures or at least listen attentively to their commentary and counsel.

The study of the Bible is more than merely reading the material. Serious study of the Bible involves the adoption of a hermeneutic. Hermeneutics is the science of literary interpretation. A student's hermeneutic sets the rules and guidelines to be used in the study. Conclusions can be no better than the hermeneutic rules that are adopted.

One basic rule of most hermeneutic systems is "Never ask the Bible to answer a question that it does not address." Such a rule should be a truism, yet it is violated over and over again. For example, the Bible cannot be asked to answer scientific questions of the 20th Century. The Bible material was written in pre-scientific eras. It is understandably silent on 20th Century understanding of chemistry, physics, biology, astronomy, or geology. My adopted hermeneutic does not allow me to ask the Bible 20th Century scientific questions.

As we approach the Bible on the subject of homosexuality, we must ask the root question: "Does the Bible in fact say anything that is applicable to the present discussion?"

Some facts are accepted by everyone. At the head of the list, Jesus said nothing on the subject. There is not a single word in the Gospels, even by inference, about any type of same-sex sexual activity. Jesus did not hesitate to comment on the evils of his day. He said nothing about homosexuality. Arguments from silence are always weak at best. Nevertheless, Jesus's silence on this particular subject is worthy of note.

Additionally, everyone agrees that there is no word in the original language of either the Old or New Testament that can be properly translated homosexual or homosexuality. There is no reference in the Bible to homosexual orientation. Apparently there is no known reference in any other extant writings of the eras of the Biblical writings. One can only conclude that male homosexual orientation was not a concern to Jesus, to the writers of the Bible materials, or to the societies in which they lived.

Whenever same-sex references are made in the Bible, it is always a reference to some particular sexual act.

I do not consider myself a Biblical scholar. I do consider myself an informed student of the Bible. My congregations have been dependent upon me to be a capable and conscientious student of the Scriptures, so that I might in turn give informed interpretations of the Scriptures to them. When the first member of my congregation said to me, "Pastor, I am gay," I became a committed student of the subject. Specifically I became committed to finding out what the Bible says about homosexuality.

Ten passages are commonly held to have some relevance to the subject:

Genesis 19 records the story of the destruction of Sodom and Gomorrah. There is no reference to homosexual activity in the passage. Two messengers from God, referred to as angels, visited Lot. Men of Sodom and Gomorrah did not want the messengers from God in their cities. They demanded Lot turn his guests over to them for sexual abuse. Lot offered his daughters instead. If the passage is any commentary about sex, it is about abuse and rape, not homosexuality. Another rule of hermeneutics is that Scripture should be allowed to comment on Scripture. Allowing Scripture to comment on Scripture, the sins of Sodom and Gomorrah were inhospitable attitude (Luke 10:10-13) and failure to care for the poor (Ezekiel 16:49-50).

Four Old Testament passages (Deuteronomy 23:17, I Kings 14:24, I Kings 22:46, and II Kings 23:7) forbid both male and female prostitution in pagan temples. The people of God were warned against selling themselves sexually for pagan religious ceremonies. A male temple prostitute performed sexual acts with another male, a clear homosexual act. I would not allow modern heterosexual prostitution to be used as a negative commentary on the morality of sexual relations between a loving husband and wife. Neither do I see any relevance of ancient male temple prostitution to the discussion of homosexuality and the practice of Christian faith in the late 20th Century.

Two more of the pertinent passages are from the Old Testament: Leviticus 18:19-23 and Leviticus 20:10-16 are a part of the Holiness Codes. The theme of the codes is summed up with "You shall be holy, for I, the Lord your God, am holy." To be holy or pure before God was something more than merely being moral. Every area of a person's life was involved. Some instructions in the Holiness Codes became central to Christian understanding. When Jesus commanded his followers to love their neighbors, he was quoting from the Holiness Codes. On the other hand, the Holiness Codes carry instructions that all Christians ignore. According to the codes, a worker must be paid his wage on the day of his labor. A field is never to be harvested to the edge. Two types of yarn are never to be woven into the same cloth. Raw meat is not to be eaten. Tattoos are forbidden. Bigamy is clearly acceptable.

Imbedded in the Holiness Codes along with an almost endless number of instructions and commands is found a prohibition of a specific homosexual act. "You shall not lie with a male as with a woman." The book of Leviticus itself gives us little help in understanding the intent of the command. Leviticus tells us nothing specific about the forbidden homosexual act. It gives us no context for the command.

Biblical scholars agree that the Holiness Codes include material that is cultural and cultic. Some material shows an understandable lack of scientific understanding. Some of the material expresses high moral sensitivity and informs all honest spiritual pursuits. What is to be done with the admonition "You shall not lie with a male as with a woman?"

Christian hermeneutics give priority to the teachings of Jesus of Nazareth over the Old Testament. Jesus set new standards for what it means to be holy. He embraced some Old Testament standards. He rejected and openly violated some other Old Testament standards: his breaking of Sabbath rules kept him in constant tension with religious leaders. He ignored some Old Testament standards. He raised justice, mercy, kindness, and love to new heights.

In the light of Jesus's life and teachings, the two Holiness Codes passages fade into obscurity and irrelevance. The Old Testament informs and instructs, but it is the New Testament and the teachings of Jesus that the Christian churches have embraced as normative and as having final authority.

It is well for hermeneutics to raise a general caution. Can any ancient prohibition set in a little known and little understood context be properly superimposed over a modern setting? In particular can the Holiness Codes statement have any relevance to the relationship between two men or two women in the 20th Century in a committed relationship that is characterized as genuinely affectionate and respectful? I think not.

This leads us to consider three passages in the New Testament. All three references about sexual deviance are found in the writings of Paul. They are Romans 1:26-2:1, I Corinthians 6:9-11, and I Timothy 1:10. These passages have always been difficult to translate and even more difficult to interpret because there are no clear English equivalents into which the key Greek words can be translated. The most exhaustive study of the issues involved was published by author Robin Scroggs in his book *The New Testament and Homosexuality*[21] published in 1983.

In his study, Scroggs takes us into the Jewish and Greek worlds of Paul's day. He researched the sexual practices and the issues of morality of that day as reflected in literature extant from that day. He found no indication of interest in same-sex sexual relationships between consenting adults. What he did find was the widespread practice of pederasty. In its usual form pederasty was a form of prostitution in which young boys were used sexually by heterosexual males. Devout Jews and Christians were understandably critical of this practice found widely among the Greeks. It is in this context that the words and expressions used by Paul are found in other literature of the same period.

It is Scroggs' argument that the three references from Paul which we have cited are not commentaries about homosexuality in general, but understandable references to the widely known practice of pederasty among the Greeks. Scroggs confronts us with another rule of hermeneutics. He maintains that for moral and ethical passages of the Bible to be applied to today's world, there must be some reasonable similarity between the contexts then and now. In this case the contexts are so dissimilar that the three passages become irrelevant. To make his point even clearer, Scroggs concludes that Paul can be shown to be against only that which he was clearly against.

One further observation is worthy of consideration. Nowhere in the New Testament is there a discussion of homosexuality or of any homosexual practice. The three New Testament references are part of lists made in the larger contexts of other discussions. Even if the importance of these three passages could be maximized and be shown to be directly relevant to today's discussion, the very incidental nature of the references would relegate them to secondary importance.

When a parishioner asks me what the Bible says about homosexuality, my most honest answer must be "Not much!"

I have expressed my best studied opinion. But I am no more than an informed student. I am not a New Testament scholar. I can ask no one to agree with me because of my standing as a scholar. I would ask that every pastor and church leader, who is serious about the issue of homosexuality and the church's ministry, take the time to sort out the facts, the fiction, the myths, the mysteries, and find a model of understanding. It is out of that model of understanding that the strangers in our midst can become our friends, our brothers and sisters in Christ.

Chapter 4

A PERSONAL INTRODUCTION

American humorist Will Rogers is reported to have said, "I have never met a man I didn't like." When we meet people and take the time to know them, disliking them becomes difficult. I suspect that is what Will Rogers was saying.

The churches' most basic problem with the gay and lesbian population is that they never meet. A homosexual's strongest coping mechanism is hiding. And hide they do. From the time gays and lesbians are teenagers, they begin hiding from their peers, their families, their teachers, their employers, and most of all, their churches. Churches are the leading spokespeople for rejection and condemnation of homosexuals. By the time they are adults, gay men and lesbians are masters of the hiding technique. In these circumstances the church never meets them. They see only a façade. As a result, churches never have an opportunity to like homosexuals, let alone love them.

My involvement with homosexuals was made easy because I began meeting them before I drew any rigid conclusions about them. I can honestly say that I have never met a gay man or a lesbian I did not like.

The homosexuals that I know are a special lot in that I have met almost all of them in some sort of pastoral or ministerial role. Almost all grew up in some religious tradition. Even though most have left their churches, they have retained spiritual sensitivities and longings.

If churches are to have meaningful ministries with homosexuals, they must meet them and take time to know them. How do we meet homosexuals? One at a time. I want you to meet some of my gay and lesbian friends. One at a time. I have changed the names and many of the circumstances in each of the following brief biographies. In their present form, they are fictional vignettes, but each describes a real person. While each person is unique, their stories and experiences are the same or similar to those of thousands, even millions more. I hope the reader will come to like them and treasure them as much as have I.

ANN

Ann is a very attractive woman. She is a classic beauty. She grew up in a small Pennsylvania town in a family most anyone would describe as normal. She dated in high school but was never serious about any of her suitors. Following high school graduation Ann took a secretarial job in a nearby college town. Tom spotted her in her place of employment. He pursued her. He was a graduate student and was about to graduate. They were married in June and moved to Alaska, where Tom had a good job offer.

Both Ann and Tom were serious Christians. Neither had any sexual experience prior to marriage. They had no financial need for Ann to work outside the home. They bought a home and over their first eight years of life together, they had four children. Every outward appearance said they were an all-American family.

Ann had no sexual interest in her husband. She was perfunctorily responsive to him. Tom accepted the situation. They cared about each other and were good parents. They had a functional family, even if not ideal.

Then Ann met Irene. Their friendship began at an adult education class. It developed into a full-fledged lesbian romance. Ann was completely ignorant of homosexuality. She just knew she felt emotionally alive, loved, and sexually stimulated.

The dynamics came to a head when Ann asked for a separate bedroom at home. Tom was distraught and later completely lost his cool when he discovered Ann had purchased an expensive gift for Irene. Irene had not set out to disrupt Ann's family. When she saw the developing chaos, she broke off the relationship with Ann. Tom decided the good of the family was best served if the marriage was preserved if at all possible. Their home is kind and gracious. Tom and Ann do a good job of parenting their children. They both understand the dynamics of their relationship and have decided to accept one another as is. They remain active in the church, but no one knows the family secret.

BEN

Ben was seventeen and a senior in high school when he called the Identity hot line. He was an excellent student and could rightfully be called artsy. His artistic talent was cultivated in high school art classes. Pen and ink was his favorite medium. Ben dressed with a flair, and when the fall chill began to descend on Anchorage, he began wearing a long black cape. He stood out in most any crowd.

Ben called the hot line to break his absolute silence about his sexual orientation. He was gay and he knew it. The hot line worker referred him to a counselor who was sympathetic. Central to Ben's anxieties was his religious training. He was certain he was condemned to hell. The counselor referred him to me knowing that I was more sympathetic. Ben had already been through pleading to God to change him into a heterosexual. He was ready for a different point of view.

Ben began attending church functions regularly. He attended a Sunday School class and joined the choir. He met other gay men but never became socially involved with them.

Ben found work in an Anchorage hotel restaurant. There he met his first love. After dating for a few months they rented an apartment together. For the first time Ben felt some inner contentment. Suddenly he disappeared. He had come out to his parents. His father, an oil field worker, shut him out. His mother was reluctantly accepting. He moved to Denver for a year. He returned to Anchorage and has settled in Girdwood. He works as a checker in a major chain store. He sees his parents occasionally. His father now accepts him, but distantly.

Ben has found a church home at the Anchorage Metropolitan Community Church. Each Sunday he drives the eighty-mile round trip to attend Sunday School and worship services. Ben enjoys the social life of the church. The minister of the church is a good pastor. Ben's spiritual needs are in capable hands.

CHARLIE

Charlie has celebrated his fortieth birthday and is a battle-scarred veteran of emotional and religious conflicts which surround his sexual orientation. Charlie's story follows some familiar patterns. He recognized his sexual interests were not those of others before junior high. Through high school he knew he was gay but had no idea what to do with his feelings. Charlie grew up in Michigan in a rigid Calvinistic family. He could intellectually move away from religious determinism, but his heart and emotions would never follow his head. His gut told him he was one of those predestined for hell.

Charlie completed three years at a private college in Michigan, Calvinist in orientation, which reinforced his early family and church training. He was thoroughly conversant with Tillich, Barth, Calvin, and Luther. He could find no resolution to the conflicts with his sexual orientation. After three years of college, he ran; first to Denver, then Seattle, and then on to

Anchorage.

Charlie had other problems. He was not particularly attractive and was considerably overweight. He had gay sexual experiences here and there, but none were in a continuing relationship. Soon after coming to Anchorage, Charlie had a schizophrenic breakdown. After hospitalization at Alaska Psychiatric Institute, he qualified for Social Security disability payments and his mental stability is maintained with medication.

In 1982 Billy Graham came to Anchorage for an evangelistic campaign. Charlie participated in every meeting. One night he responded to the invitation. He poured out his guilt and shame to a counselor. Counselors fervently prayed over him. His deliverance from homosexuality was reported on the front page of the Anchorage daily paper. For six months he felt free of his homosexual impulses. Then they came back. He prayed with great agony. After several weeks of struggle, Charlie accepted that he was a homosexual.

Over the next two years, Charlie was delivered from homosexuality three more times. Twice he was delivered in charismatic churches and once in a more Calvinistic setting. Each time his homosexual impulses returned.

Charlie is stable on his medication. He is unable to work. He accepts his homosexuality. He attends a very conservative independent church that holds to Calvinistic teaching. No one at his church knows of his homosexuality. He is not sexually involved with anyone, male or female.

DEVON

Devon was the oldest of five children. His mother is a jovial lady, who is much loved by her children. Devon's father is a retired Alaska State Trooper. Devon's parents were divorced but not until he was an engineering student at Washington State University. He maintained a positive relationship with his parents, and took particular care to see that his mother's needs were met.

Devon was a goodlooking man. There was no hint of being gay in his body movement, manners, or voice. As a teenager he was unsure of himself socially, but he always managed to have a date for all the big school events. At Washington State, he became more aware of homosexuality and affirmed what he already knew. He was gay. There was a sizable gay and lesbian population at the University. He became part of gay social life. He did some partying which included heavy drinking and sexual orgies.

After graduating from Washington State, Devon returned to Anchorage. He got an engineering job with one of the major oil companies and settled in to build a career. He was an able and well-paid engineer.

In the summer Devon played softball, volleyball in the winter. He played softball for one of the teams sponsored by his employer. While playing ball, Devon met Roger. After a cautious friendship, they acknowledged their sexual orientation to each other and fell deeply in love. They moved in together. Later they bought a very large and beautiful condominium. While they never exchanged commitments to each other in a formal service, they were lifetime partners.

At work their relationship was in the closet. Even though they worked in the same building, they drove separate cars to work and rarely ate lunch together. When Devon attended church, he always came alone. In the church guest register his address was never more than a post office box number. His phone number was his work number.

Four years after Devon and Roger bought their condo, Devon began developing sores on his skin. They were the telltale signs of AIDS-related cancer. He lost weight rapidly and his death was kind in that the process was not prolonged. His funeral was a private service. The service was led by a minister who never knew him. He was buried on a family-owned plot of ground in the Alaska Interior. Roger tests HIV positive but shows no signs of illness. He and Devon's mother now attend the church pastored by the minister who conducted Devon's funeral.

ED AND FRANK

Ed and Frank are a couple. They have been together for fourteen years. Both are out of the closet to everyone. They obviously enjoy one another. They do not hesitate to hold hands or embrace in public. They are very supportive of one another.

Ed is the son of a Protestant minister. He knew he was gay from junior high school, but faithfully played the heterosexual game through high school. He was handsome then. He still is but could stand to lose fifty pounds to look his best. He is not effeminate in any way. He is very verbal and is as smooth with words as he is prolific. He modestly claims the girls chased him incessantly in earlier days.

Ed left home to go to junior college. Here he came out of the closet and had his first same-sex experience. The next step was to get out of the closet with his parents, his brother, and his sister. They were all accepting, and Ed felt more free to be who he was.

College was not for Ed, and after one year he moved to Anchorage where his father had accepted a pastorate. There was lots of building going on in Anchorage, and Ed decided he wanted to be a carpenter. He completed an apprenticeship and enjoyed the trade. He was good at detail work and started doing finish carpentering. Ed was never a performer, but he loved the theater and enjoyed being around the theater crowd. His skills were soon discovered and he became very valuable to theater groups around Anchorage as a set builder. While building a set for one of the Anchorage theater groups, Ed met Frank.

Frank was small. His speech was affected. Many of his mannerisms were effeminate. He wore some strange clothes combinations. He was the most creative set designer in town. Frank was the son of a successful Connecticut lawyer. The family was Catholic, and Frank's mother was socially active. She took special interest in local theater groups. Frank was always small for his age. His father wanted him to be a man. He took piano lessons and loved it. By the time Frank was in high school, his appearance was less than masculine. Father was not pleased.

Frank went off to college at a good Catholic university. He majored in art and quickly became a part of gay social life on campus. Frank's mother suspected he was gay, but it was never a matter of family discussion. Frank was a junior when he brought a boyfriend home at spring break. When he "outed" himself to his parents, his mother cried buckets of tears, but accepted reality. His father was horrified. He ranted and raved about the disgrace of having a queer son.

Theater had become Frank's true love. He completed a Master's degree in theater with an emphasis on set design. Then he ran as far from home as he could. He ran all the way to Anchorage, Alaska.

There was lots of money for theater in those days. Frank's move to Alaska was timed perfectly. He found work and was well paid for his efforts.

Since both Ed and Frank were very open about their sexual orientation, it was not difficult for them to get together. After a whirlwind romance, they moved in together and declared themselves a couple. They bought a condominium and settled down.

Ed decided he wanted to return to college. That was fine with Frank. They had savings and Frank had good income. Three years later Ed had his degree in political science. He completed the additional work which is required in Alaska to qualify for a teaching certificate.   He works as a substitute teacher in the public schools of Anchorage.

Ed likes substitute teaching because it allows him time to be a gay rights activist.   He also is active in state party politics. He is interested in many political issues other than gay rights. His goal is election to the State legislature.

One note of interest.   Ed's father recently retired from the ministry.   Even though he had been privately accepting of his son's sexual orientation, he never publicly acknowledged his son's gay orientation nor spoke out for justice for homosexuals until his last sermon.   Such is the fear that grips ministers.

GENE

Gene was one of two children and an only son.   His parents divorced when he was preschool age.   His father was a career military officer, and Gene saw very little of him as he grew up.   His mother was a devout Catholic and reared her children in the Church.   They attended parochial schools, practiced their faith conscientiously, and never missed mass.

Gene's mother wanted grandchildren and kept pressure on him to marry his high school sweetheart.   He became a sales representative for a cosmetics company and, to his mother's delight, married.   Gene did so fully realizing he was gay.   He was still closeted, having told no one.   The marriage was a disaster. He divorced and ran from his native Florida.

The next stop was Denver.   He entered beauty school, supporting himself waiting tables.   He became a hairdresser, became a part of the gay bar scene, and became heavily involved with alcohol and drugs.   Gene's first try to live as a gay man was a total disaster.   He ran again—to Anchorage, Alaska.

As a teenager Gene had worked at restaurants as a dishwasher, then as a busboy, and eventually did some cooking. He was very personable, and in Anchorage he talked himself into a job as night manager of the Village Inn Restaurant. He took a genuine interest in his staff and did very well. He decided to give heterosexuality another try. He began dating one of the waitresses, and the two began attending a Protestant Church. They decided to move into an apartment together for economic reasons. They had separate bedrooms and never slept together. Gene simply could not function sexually with a woman.

Gene's mother was delighted to hear her son was involved with a woman, but Gene could not stand the pressure. He began drinking and using drugs again. He fell apart. Apparently he went through some sort of psychotic break. Friends took him with glassy eyes and incoherent speech to Alaska Psychiatric Institute. As soon as they could stabilize him, Gene was shipped home to his mother in Florida.

In a few months Gene stabilized and returned to Anchorage. He became a car salesman. He was very good at selling and was rolling in the commissions. He gave up trying to be heterosexual once and for all. He became active in gay activities in Anchorage. He returned to heavy use of cocaine.

Gene developed a heavy cough. When he went to see his doctor, he discovered he tested HIV positive. He had more than a cough. He had AIDS-related pneumonia. Gene moved back to Florida to be near his family.

HESTER

Hester is a high profile leader in the Anchorage lesbian population. Under the fire of reporters and the presence of television cameras, she is cool and articulate. Almost anyone would be impressed when meeting Hester. She is feminine in appearance. She dresses conservatively. She speaks precisely about a range of issues with no rancor in her voice and a smile on her face.

Hester was reared in a devout Roman Catholic family in Upstate New York. She accepted her sexual orientation in high school, but did not make it known until she was in college. She became an outspoken feminist and renounced Catholicism. She did not perceive this as leaving the Christian faith. Her family was reluctantly accepting of their non-conforming member. Because of the encouragement of a friend, following graduation Hester moved to Anchorage. Very quickly she became active in both feminist and lesbian organizations.

Finding employment was no problem. Hester was hired by a non-profit organization that ran large programs for children. She was a hit with the children, and it did not take long for her organizational abilities to be recognized. She became the director of one of the programs. Not only did the children love her, parents liked her as well. The executive director gave her the highest of ratings in her evaluations. Hester became one of the most valued employees in the organization.

Even after two years, Hester's executive director had not become aware of her sexual orientation or her growing activism in Anchorage. Then she marched in the annual Gay Pride parade. As fate would have it, her picture was on the front page of the Sunday edition of the local newspaper. Her executive director had the picture in hand when she was called into his office on Monday morning. During the prior week, he had met with Hester to go over his latest annual review of her work. She had been given the highest possible marks. But now he was alarmed. He was concerned about the safety of the children they served. He was fearful of the possible reaction of parents who used their services. Hester pointed out that she was still the same person who had left work on Friday with her director's full confidence.

The relationship between Hester and her director became cool and filled with tension. Hester did not want to work under those conditions and began looking for other employment. She found work with an agency that served mentally ill adults. Her sexual orientation did not bother her new employer. She continues to be a good employee who brings genuine caring to her work.

Alaska brought important relationships to Hester. She met Dianne at a lesbian social event. They began dating and then moved in together. Dianne drives a delivery truck. She had been involved in a heterosexual marriage and had an eight-year-old daughter. After the divorce Dianne received custody of her daughter and her ex-husband left Alaska. Dianne has little of the sophistication of Hester. She was not raised with any religious tradition. She drives an old pickup with questionable dependability. The threesome riding in the old pickup always appears to be a happy group.

About a year after they moved in together, Hester and Dianne decided they wanted their relationship blessed. I officiated at their service of blessing in the church's prayer chapel in the presence of close friends. They have now celebrated their seventh anniversary. Dianne's daughter is in junior high. They have been active in Girl Scouts and PTA. They hide their relationship from no one. They have visited some churches but have not found a place where they can be themselves.

ISAAC

I never met Isaac face to face. Ours was entirely a phone relationship. The relationship was obviously important to him since he continued calling me. I never once called him; I never had his phone number. This is Isaac's story.

Isaac was raised in a Southern Baptist family in Tulsa, Oklahoma. His family was loving and stable. His sister and two brothers were "saved" in late grade school or junior high years. Isaac accepted the Lord when he was eleven. His parents were very active in the church. It was a model Southern Baptist family. Isaac's faith was genuine. He embraced everything his church taught. He believed the Bible was the word of God and was to be interpreted literally. During his whole lifetime, Isaac had attended Sunday School, morning worship, Training Union, Sunday evening service, and mid-week Bible study and prayer service. He had willingly served any committee or board responsibility offered to him. During the period of our phone conversations, he was serving on his church's Board of Deacons.

About the same time Isaac was saved, he started to become aware of his sexual interest in other boys. In the same process he became aware that he did not have any particular interest in girls. Through high school years he dated girls and always was able to fit into the social circles of both church and school. Homosexuality was never discussed in any of his social settings. He loved music and sang in his church's youth choir and the choirs at his high school. He graduated from high school puzzled about sex but without any sexual experience, homosexual or heterosexual.

Isaac's next step was Oklahoma State University. In high school he had done well in math and sciences. At OSU he became a botany major. He loved growing things. His experiments were not work; they were a joy. The social focus of Isaac's four years at OSU was the Baptist Student Union. His dating was heterosexual, but he was not sexually active. As he neared graduation, he became engaged to the girl he had been dating. She was also active in BSU. They were married in June following graduation, and family, church, and friends were happy for this ideal Christian couple.

Isaac decided his long-range goal was to own a floral shop. He had taken courses in floral design and loved it. He began working in a floral shop and his dual life began. At home he and his wife began a family and eventually had two children. At work he became sexually involved with a young man who was more experienced than he. He finally admitted to himself what he had feared for several years. He was homosexual. He wept for God's grace after each homosexual experience. At home he was a good father and a kind husband. This first phase of his double life lasted eleven years. His wife became ill and died of cancer.

In the eyes of his church Isaac was a businessman who had been left a widow with two children to raise. He continued to be active in his church. He sang in the choir and taught junior high youth in Sunday School. His hidden life as an active homosexual also continued.

Through his gay social contacts, Isaac met a lesbian whose friendship he enjoyed. She also had strong needs to remain closeted. She too was a Southern Baptist and her faith was important to her. She and Isaac decided to enter into a marriage of convenience.

With a new marriage, Isaac, wife, and two children moved to Anchorage where he purchased a floral shop. Isaac and his wife not only finished rearing Isaac's two children, they also adopted two Vietnamese refugee children and raised them. During their years in Anchorage, they remained active in their Southern Baptist Church and both had homosexual lovers. They never wavered from their conservative Southern Baptist beliefs. Each time their pastors and their church friends would speak condemningly about homosexuals, they would cringe and go through another bout of guilt.

Why would Isaac call me having lived through over thirty years of living his dual life? Isaac discovered he tested HIV positive. Was this God's judgment? How would Isaac tell his family in Oklahoma? What would he tell them? Should he stay in Anchorage? Was there any safe place for Isaac? When I moved to the Matanuska Valley, I lost contact with Isaac. I have no idea what has happened to him.

JOY

Joy's bubbly personality belied the intensity of the pain she has felt over her thirty-three years. Possessed with good looks as well as a pleasing personality, she was a person in social demand through her grade school and high school years. Boys and girls sought her out, but her response was always cautious because she did not want anyone to know what was going on inside her. Joy was sexually attracted to girls not boys.

While in junior high school, Joy found an interest that absorbed her emotions and her energies: the cello. She became an accomplished cellist and played in the Anchorage Junior Symphony and later the Anchorage Symphony. In high school she had one brief sexual encounter with a butch classmate. She found the relationship frightening and withdrew into herself and her guilt. She felt something was terribly wrong with her, and she found no help with her dilemma.

At age nineteen, Joy was pursued by a young man who turned out to be a heavy drinker and an abuser. She saw the signals before they married. She married him anyway. She cannot explain why she married other than she wanted to be "normal." Joy was not sexually responsive to her husband and always blamed herself when he drank and abused her. A son was born. When he was just over a year old, Joy escaped this marriage with a restraining order in hand.

Joy did not have an employable skill that could support her and her son. Welfare and food stamps were the next step. She met Dave through a mutual friend.   He was quiet, hardworking, had a good job, and adored Joy's son who was now two years old. He treated Joy with genuine kindness. When he proposed marriage, she was honest and told him of her sexual orientation.   With no understanding of the homosexual phenomenon, he assured her that it made no difference. Everything would be okay. He was sure they could overcome any problems and have a good marriage. Joy decided Dave was the best chance for a stable life for her and her son.

Two more children were born, both boys. It was a robust family when I met them at a funeral. Joy was aware of me even though we had never met. A few days later she called me and asked me to visit her. When I met with her she came right to the point. "I am lesbian." At this point their marriage not only looked good from the outside, it had some real strengths. Joy and Dave were kind and considerate of one another. They enjoyed parenting the children. They were good parents. Dave loved music as much as did Joy. Their home was full of music. But there was the other side. Joy had a relationship with another woman. It was exciting and satisfying. Dave knew of the other person but was tolerant. Eventually Joy concluded that it was best for her marriage and family to break off the relationship and had done so. Now she was feeling a strong pull back to her lover. She was trying to be warm toward Dave but found it impossible to relate to him as anything but a good friend.

Joy's children are all in grade school, and she has begun working outside the home. With the help of a counselor, Joy and Dave have set some long-term goals. They are staying together. They would like to buy a place with acreage, raise dogs, and become serious mushers. Joy would like some day to run the Iditarod.**

KEN

Ken is one of the three closest gay friends I have had. I

**The Iditarod is a sled-dog race from Anchorage to Nome. The name refers to the gold mining town on the trail. The distance is 1,049 miles. The race begins in March of every year.

first met him when I was a junior in college and he was in first or second grade. As a financially struggling college student, I picked up all the odd job work I could through the employment office run by the college. One Saturday I was sent to the home of Ken's family. His father was a successful Chicago businessman. Their suburban home was very large and rambling and was set on a few acres the family still calls "the ranch." The home had to be large to accommodate the size of the family. Ken had eight brothers and a sister. Ken was just one of the kids who were around that day as I worked cleaning and repairing an old chicken house. We laughed 30 years later when we pieced our stories together and realized we had met before.

My wife, Darlene, and I had gone out for coffee with friends at Bob's Big Boy in Anchorage. I noticed one of two men in the next booth listening to our conversation about church and spiritual concerns. They left the restaurant, but one returned in a few minutes. It was Ken. He asked if I was a minister. As we chatted, I indicated I was a graduate of Wheaton College in what turned out to be his home town, Wheaton, Illinois. We exchanged business cards and went our separate ways. He called and a close friendship began.

Ken was small but very athletic. He kept physically active and pumped a little iron at one of the local health clubs. He always had a smile on his face and usually wore a navy blue baseball cap with gold scrambled eggs on the bill. He was a handsome man.

Ken had stayed in the Chicago area through his college years. He was an excellent wrestler and had won many honors in high school and college. While in college he was a part of the Reserve Officers Training Corps, and upon graduation, Ken went on active duty as a Second Lieutenant in the Army. The Vietnam War was in full swing and the Army needed helicopter pilots. He volunteered and a year later was flying helicopters over the jungles of Vietnam. He survived his one-year tour of duty and was discharged when he completed his active duty obligation to the Army.

The flying bug had bitten. He began taking flying lessons in fixed wing aircraft with the goal of becoming a commercial airline pilot. Ken passed the necessary tests as rapidly as was allowed and spent all the time he could building up hours of flight time. He made it. Ken became first an engineer and then co-pilot for a major airline. He flew western routes that included Alaska. To the casual observer, Ken was an All-American success story.

But there was the other side of the story.

By the time Ken reached high school, he realized he was sexually different. His family's conservative beliefs and church taught him that his same-sex feelings were wrong and that there was something terribly wrong with him. During high school and college he played the heterosexual game. His athletic reputation, his good looks, and a charming personality made it easy to play the game. Ken did not become homosexually active until after his college years. He had shared with no one his homosexual orientation during high school and college. During his Army years he began living a double life. He was homosexually active, but also dated a woman from the time of his army flight training. She waited for him while he served in Vietnam. When he returned, they married.

Ken made a valiant attempt to be heterosexual. His marriage became one more part of the image of the American success story. Eventually he found himself living a double life. Seattle became the home base for his work as an airline pilot. When at home in Seattle, Ken was a married man, church active, and an airline pilot. Away from home when he had an overnight layovers in other cities, he was a promiscuous homosexual.

The marriage lasted five years. Ken moved to Anchorage and began flying second seat in 727s for a different airline. In a sense Ken continued living a double life. Airlines are very tolerant of gay and lesbian flight attendants, but a gay pilot is not acceptable. At work he kept himself in a closet with the door very tightly closed.

Ken was hard working and ambitious. Over the years he had learned construction skills. In Anchorage he began buying bargain properties that were run down. He and Brad, his partner-lover, rebuilt the properties, sometimes keeping them, sometimes selling them. His flying schedule gave him blocks of free time, and he made good use of them. To stay busy in the winter, he started a snowplowing business. For additional summer work, he started a landscape construction and maintenance business.

At our second luncheon date, Ken began telling me of his painful history. We found that we not only had common friendships in Wheaton but also in the Anchorage gay population. Ken had dropped out of church life but had never forsaken his love of God and God's Savior Son.

Ken became a regular church attender. In the winter he plowed the church parking lot but never sent a bill. He made a generous donation toward the construction of a prayer chapel in the church building. He could never, however, bring himself to join the membership of the church. At best he remained a fringe participant.

After his divorce Ken had come out of the closet to his family with mixed response. His father had already died not knowing the family secret. His mother was disturbed but never turned her back on her son. From his brothers and sister, he got a mixed review. His mother was always Ken's special concern. She made regular visits to Anchorage, and it was always special when Ken, his mother, and Brad worshipped together.

Ken came to my office and spoke the painful words, "I have AIDS." Brad also tested HIV positive. They had been tested after Brad seemed to have a chest cold he could not shake. Ken showed no signs of illness as yet. He had made up his mind about how best to care for his partner. AIDS medical expertise in Anchorage was limited. He and Brad moved to Southern California. Ken began flying for a commuter airline and was based at John Wayne Airport in Orange County. Brad deteriorated very quickly and died of AIDS-related pneumonia.

Before learning of their HIV infection, Ken and Brad had purchased a run-down home on property overlooking Puget Sound in Washington state. They vacationed there occasionally, but their goal was to completely renovate the place into their dream retirement home. After Brad died, Ken quit his flying job and moved to the old house on Puget Sound and began the reconstruction. He made trips to Anchorage to see his friends. On one of those trips I spotted the tell-tale cancerous lesions and recognized his weight loss. He worked on the house as long as he had strength. The task was never completed. He died in Seattle in 1991.

LARRY

Larry's story is short because, unfortunately, his life was short. Larry's family moved to Anchorage when he was a freshman in high school. It was obvious he was adopted because he was Asian and his parents were of European ancestry. They had adopted him as an infant. The parents were quite conservative. The family attended church but never really became a part of it. They seemed to be attracted to the church but could not feel comfortable with what they perceived as liberal tendencies. The pastor's overt acceptance of homosexuals was specifically upsetting.

Larry came to some activities of the church youth group but never made close friends. He was outwardly friendly and even gregarious, but he never allowed anyone to be close to him. In school he was an excellent student. He showed some interest in the guitar but soon set it aside. He took up running and was good enough to be a varsity cross country runner.

After graduating from an Anchorage high school, Larry entered the University of Washington. He completed one year and did well academically. After the one year, he decided to enroll in the University of Alaska Anchorage.

Late on an August Friday night, the Anchorage police noticed a lone car in the parking lot at one of the municipal parks. The motor was running. They found Larry sitting in the driver's seat dead. He had run a hose from the car's exhaust into the car and closed the windows.

The family grief was enormous. There was no note. There was no indication of what might have been troubling their son. Through gay friends in Anchorage I learned Larry was gay. He had shared that he could never tell anyone in his family. He became a teenage statistic.

MARIE

Marie is so special because she has tried so hard to love God and has sought so desperately to be assured that God loves her.

Marie is an only child born to a schizophrenic mother, who never married. Marie has never known her father or anything about him. Her mother was able to work only occasionally. She and Marie were able to survive on various forms of public assistance.

Marie's base of stability was the public school system. She was bright and always did well in school. She had girl friends at school but never felt free to bring them to her home. Her mother and the disarray of her home was a closely guarded secret. The goals of her life became set very early—keep her secrets and survive.

Marie's ability to survive was put to a severe test when she was ten years old. Her mother was hospitalized for several months. Somehow Marie fell through the cracks of the social services system. When she ran out of food and money and the rent was unpaid, she became a street person. Incredibly she survived an entire Alaskan winter in Anchorage. She slept in empty buildings or anywhere she could find shelter. She stayed in school and actually continued to be a good student. With some regularity she would work out an overnight or a weekend stay with a girl friend.   Two thoughts ran through her mind—survival and suicide. She survived.

Marie's mother was eventually released from the hospital, and mother and daughter were reunited. They lived on public assistance and Marie, for all practical purposes, became the parent of her mother.

Through a girl friend, Marie and her mother began attending an Anchorage charismatic church. The atmosphere was exciting and free. They both embraced a newfound Christian faith. Even though her mother remained unstable, Marie's teen years in the church were some of the best in her whole life. But it was also during these years that she began realizing she had no sexual attraction for men but rather was drawn to intimate relationships with women. At first she tried to change her feelings through her relationship with God. It did not work, and Marie realized she was one of those homosexuals against whom her church regularly railed. She drifted away from the church even though her mother remained.

Marie continued her education beyond high school graduation. She was good at math and enjoyed numbers. She completed junior college with a degree in bookkeeping. Marie had no difficulty finding employment and eventually she became a full charge bookkeeper for a small Anchorage firm. She continues in that position and does well financially.

Having drifted away from her church, finished college, and gained solid employment, Marie started looking for social outlets. She became a part of the Anchorage lesbian network of communities.   She volunteered time to gay and lesbian organizations and causes, but there was always the care of her mother in the background. She continued to long to be part of a church.

One of Marie's closest friends was Jim, a gay man she met through her gay and lesbian social life. He was also a friend of mine.   Marie and Jim dated with some regularity.   They enjoyed one another's company and dating served as an effective cover for both of them. Neither of them was out of the closet at work. Jim was Roman Catholic and attended mass regularly. Marie went to mass with him a few times but could not tune in to that style of worship.   Jim told Marie about me and the church I pastored.   One Sunday morning they appeared in worship service. They were greeted warmly, and Marie felt at home. I had lunch with Marie. She was excited. She knew she had found a church home.

When she joined the membership of the church, in her enthusiasm, Marie told the Deacons that she was lesbian and happy to find a church that welcomed her as the person she was. While other gay and lesbian people had joined the church, Marie was the first who had been completely open to the Deacon Board. They handled it well, and Marie loved the church.

When I resigned from the pastorate and other leadership came, Marie no longer felt welcome and quietly left.   For a second time a cherished church relationship was lost. I referred her to another minister who serves as an institutional chaplain. The two have become close friends, but Marie is still without a church home. She lives with her lover in a blessed relationship. She still looks after her mother, who has been stabilized on medication. Marie's thoughts about suicide have returned, but she has been able to handle them with the help of her chaplain.

NORM

Growing up gay in a devoutly Pentecostal family in a small town in Tennessee was not easy, especially when two of your three older brothers were ordained preachers. That was Norm's lot. His father was a mechanic at the local Ford dealer and life revolved around church and cars. Cars didn't frighten Norm, but the guys who loved to have their hands in grease frightened him to a point of panic. This was the same crowd that was as hung up on girls as they were on cars. Norm found a way out. He became as hung up on music and religion as others were on cars and girls.

Even before Norm first realized that he was different, he was attracted to the piano. He begged for lessons, and his parents responded. Norm spent hours practicing. It was difficult to tear him away from the piano for family meals. By the time he was in junior high, he was playing for all the music groups at school, and he became a star performer at his church. He could read music. He could improvise. He could turn a hymn into jazz, blues, or even rock and roll. And he was seriously religious. He loved Jesus with his whole heart.

By the time Norm entered high school, he knew for sure that he was homosexual. But he knew of no one else who was. The preacher at his church made the sinfulness of being gay a regular topic. Norm spent a lot of time at the altar crying out to God in repentance, but never let anyone know the truth of his repentance. He begged God to be changed and nothing happened. The more he ached inside the more fervently he threw himself into his music. Music was Norm's passion, and it was also his escape. During his high school years he had no sexual involvements, homosexual or heterosexual. This all changed when he settled into the music department at the University of Tennessee. Within the department were other students who were openly gay. While he was never what he deemed promiscuous, during his university days Norm was seriously involved in three different gay relationships. At the same time he remained very active in a local Pentecostal church. He lived a double life. He was open to no one in either his church or his family.

Upon graduation Norm answered an ad for a high school music teacher on the Kenai Peninsula in Southcentral Alaska. He moved to Alaska and settled into a career as a music teacher that lasted fifteen years. He became choir director at a local Pentecostal church. While in Alaska he was never open with anyone. It was a different matter when he vacationed. He traveled widely, sometimes with gay tour groups. He traveled to England, Europe, Japan, and Australia. He visited his hometown and his family only for brief periods of time. When away from Alaska, church, and family, Norm was very promiscuous.

Toward the end of the last year of his teaching, Norm had a chest cold he could not shake. Tests showed him to be HIV positive. He applied for a one-year leave of absence and moved to Anchorage. He was directed to the church I pastored. He attended services regularly and joined the choir. He deteriorated rapidly and was hospitalized. To this point his family knew nothing of his sexual orientation or his full blown case of AIDS. Now he wanted to be reunited with his family. He was too weak to write and asked me to write his oldest brother who was pastor of a Pentecostal church in Southern California. I wrote, making a plea that Norm be accepted with Christian grace. Arrangements were made, and he was transferred to a Los Angeles hospital. I received a note from his brother. His family had all gathered in Southern California to be with Norm. He deteriorated rapidly and died. According to his brother, Norm repented of his homosexuality before he died and died in peace.

OLLIE

Ollie was an organization man in gay circles. He was the best connected man in gay circles that I have known. He knew who was who. He knew what was going on. I got to know him during the years I was active on the Board of Directors of Identity, Inc. He was a volunteer for every project and was very dependable. If money was needed, he gave. It was he who thought I needed to see the inside of gay bars. He took me on a tour and with seeming delight introduced his non-drinking, non-gay Baptist minister friend.

Ollie was no longer interested in religion, or so he said. He seemed to enjoy our friendship. I suspected he valued being connected with religion, even if it was only through a friendship. Ollie was an angry and somewhat bitter ex-Roman Catholic. Now in his early forties, he had waved "good-bye" to the Catholic Church some twenty years earlier. Being gay was the only issue. He couldn't reconcile his church and his sexual orientation. He chose to be faithful to his sexual orientation.

I never talked to Ollie about how he got to Alaska. He was from Massachusetts. I suspect that after choosing gayness over religion and after graduating from college, he ran away, and Alaska is far away. Ollie had become a government bureaucrat and worked as an office supervisor. He was not out of the closet at work, but there were some in the office he felt suspected that he was gay. He felt constant tensions with two people in his office, one being his supervisor.

A complaint was filed against Ollie's management style. About the same time the complaint was filed, Ollie decided to march in the Gay Pride parade. It was the first time for him, as it was for me. The last thing he wanted was to be photographed by the news media. We walked together the whole way. When Ollie spotted someone with a camera, he would step over so I was between him and the camera. It did not work. The next

112

day the Anchorage paper carried a picture in which Ollie was the most prominent subject. I was neatly tucked behind him.

The following Monday, copies of the picture were passed through the office and posted on the bulletin board. Ollie learned later that a copy was sent to his department head in Juneau, the state capital. Word got back to him that his supervisor vowed to "get that fag." It was in that context that Ollie had his hearing on the complaint filed against him. His union representative advised Ollie that there was insufficient evidence against him and nothing was in his personnel file. As a result of the hearing, Ollie was given six months to improve his management style. He complied and continued in his supervisory position.

About a year later the office was reorganized. Under the reorganization two supervisors were needed at Ollie's level rather than three. Even though Ollie had more seniority than the other two supervisors, it was Ollie's job that was eliminated. He was reduced in employment level. He decided not to fight it. He knew what had happened.

As good a friend as Ollie was, I did not really know him. If he was in a long-term relationship, it was hidden. I have no idea where he lived. I suspected he drank too much. Ollie seemed to know everyone. I doubt if he ever let anyone know him.

PETE

Pete grew up in the church. His parents were two of the most active persons in the congregation. She sang in the choir, taught Sunday School. Pete's father served on the Church board. He was middle level management in one of the area's research and development companies. When in high school, he was a better than average football player. He had not pursued athletics in college but was an avid fan. As Pete grew up, his father prepped him constantly to become an athlete. His stout, husky build pointed him to football.

Pete worked hard at being a football player and became good enough at the sport to play varsity for his high school during his junior and senior years. As I watched Pete mature, something did not ring true. He played football, but never seemed to really care for the game. Just as soon as football season was over, he was trying out for parts in plays and musicals. The chairman of the performing arts department was known to be gay. I also knew other students active in the theater program who I suspected were gay or lesbian.

Pete's mother spoke to me about her son. The family was pleased with his success in school (he was also an excellent student), but she was bewildered about his behavior at home. He had become very withdrawn. He spent little time with the family. He spent hours in his room playing the guitar. He was teaching himself and practiced every day for hours at a time.

I added two and two and jumped to a precarious and tentative conclusion. I suspected Pete was gay. I did not discuss this with his parents. I called Pete and made an after school date. I picked him up and we went out for a sundae. Chit-chat about school and his latest acting role was easy enough. The hard part was bringing up his sexual orientation. I plunged in. "Pete, I suspect you are gay. If I am wrong, and you are in any way offended, I apologize. If I am correct, I want you to know that it is all right to be gay. God's love and acceptance of you is just the same as for a non-gay person. If I can be of any help to you as you sort this out, it would be my privilege."

An awkward silence followed. Pete never confirmed or denied my suspicion. He thanked me for my concern and changed the subject.

Pete graduated from high school that June, and in the fall he entered a church-related college in California with a strong music department. He continued to be an excellent student and became a fine musician. He rarely came home during the school year and found summer jobs away from home.

The summer following his sophomore year I was walking in the downtown area and heard a voice yell "Pastor Bess!" I turned to see Pete running toward me. He grabbed me and hugged me with a long and tight hug. He explained he was in a hurry but just wanted to say "Hi." The long embrace said more than words. We both understood the message.

The last I heard about Pete was that he was playing lead guitar for a rock band that was soon leaving on a European tour.

QUINCY

Quin is a fellow American Baptist minister. He was especially helpful to me because he was the first person who took the time to explain the inner turmoil experienced by a gay man, especially one who believed he was called to be a minister of the gospel.

Quin was raised in an American Baptist church in Southern California by parents who were about as committed to Christ and the church as one could imagine. He was loved by pastors, Sunday School teachers, and youth leaders. He embraced the faith of his parents and church from the time he was a child. Quin was baptized when in junior high. When in high school he attended a summer camp at Thousand Pines Baptist Conference Center in the San Bernardino Mountains and felt God called him to be a minister. He never wavered from that call. After high school graduation Quin enrolled at the University of Redlands, an American Baptist-related college. Next came Berkeley Baptist Divinity School (now American Baptist Seminary of the West). Immediately following completion of divinity school, he was ordained. He was bright, talented, goodlooking, and committed.

Outwardly the path of Quin's journey appeared healthy

and trouble free. This did not match what was going on inside of him. Back in junior high he had begun to realize he was different. Girls liked him and let him know. As he went through high school he did all the right things socially. He enjoyed the company of girls and dated often. But it was plain to him that his interest lay with boys, not girls. At Redlands he knew that he was a queer, a fag, a fairy. He suspected others around him were also, but he stayed in the closet for those four years with the door tightly closed. It was at Berkeley in a dorm prayer meeting that Quin first shared his torment. The response was a laying on of hands and fervent prayers. His same-sex desires seemed to disappear, and Quin was sure he had been healed of his terrible malady. The feelings came back. There were more prayer meetings. After each prayer meeting the period of feeling free seemed to last longer.

Near the end of his last year in seminary, Quin decided he should marry. He had been dating Rose somewhat regularly for two years. He proposed marriage. Rose said yes. They were married the week following graduation. Just prior to the marriage, all the old homosexual feelings came surging back. He was in a state of panic, but he went through with the marriage anyway.

The marriage of Quin and Rose lasted sixteen years. Three children were born to the marriage. Quin served four years as an associate minister in an American Baptist church and pastored two other American Baptist churches for a total of twelve years. Rose was killed in an auto accident.

During all the years of struggle, Quin had not had a single homosexual sexual encounter. He had been completely faithful to Rose during their sixteen-year marriage. Now he was a widow with three junior and senior high children to raise. About a year after the death of Rose, Quin met Tom. They became lovers, but their relationship was tightly closeted. The Stonewall Inn incident took place and hit the papers. Quin and

Tom took courage and decided to come out of the closet. Quin made his homosexuality known to his congregation. When he realized the intensity of their negative reaction, he resigned. He was not able to find further employment as a minister in American Baptist churches or any other denomination. Tom moved in with Quin and they finished rearing Quin's children.

Eventually Quin became a marriage and family counselor. He is now retired. He and Tom are still together.

RUBY

Ruby knew she was lesbian when she married Harry, but her life had been so hectic, she was looking for some stability. Her mother died when she was eleven, and her alcoholic father disappeared two years later. She and an older sister tried to make it on their own. They couldn't. Ruby lived most of the next four years in foster homes. None of them were all that great. She found herself almost eighteen, a high school graduate, and on her own. The only job she could find was waitressing at a Denny's restaurant.

Harry was a shy, somewhat introverted student at a California State University campus. He hung out at Denny's. Ruby was very friendly and aggressively so with Harry. She was not yet nineteen when Harry graduated with a degree in business and they were married. Jobs were not plentiful at the time, and Harry joined the Air Force. After basic training, he was sent to Vandenberg Air Force Base where he spent the remainder of his four-year enlistment. Both of Ruby and Harry's children were born at Vandenberg. Upon discharge Harry went to work for a large Southern California grocery chain.

There were two things Harry never could figure out. Ruby had very little interest in sex, and she always seemed to have a close girl friend with whom she spent a lot of time. The first time Ruby asked if he cared if she took an extended

117

vacation with her friend, he was not enthusiastic but assented. Over the next few years this became a pattern. Harry lost himself in work and a variety of sports interests.

Harry was doing well at work, handled his money carefully, and invested in property. He was doing very well. Ruby decided to go to the local junior college to become a dental technician. Upon completion of her training, she had no trouble finding a well-paying job.

Ruby's next step was to propose construction of a second home in a recreational area about forty miles away. Money was no problem. She designed the house, made all the business arrangements, and supervised the construction. However, Harry was a bit taken aback when Ruby asked that the new house be placed in her name only. It was then that Harry came to me trying to figure things out.

I listened and asked if Ruby could possibly be lesbian. Harry had never even thought of such a dynamic. When Harry confronted Ruby, she readily admitted that he had finally guessed correctly. She insisted, however, that she did not want a divorce. Harry decided he did.

Ruby lives in the new second home. She is active in a nearby church. She still maintains her close female friendships and still goes on vacations with her special friend.

Harry has remarried and is very happy.

SAM

I cannot imagine Sam without a smile on his face. I first met him at the counter of the local post office. He was a clerk, and I was a customer. When I saw him playing the organ at the funeral of a prominent Anchorage gay leader, he seemed so very familiar. Speaking with him following the service, together we figured out the past contact. It was the beginning of a long and close friendship.

Sam was raised a Southern Baptist in Florida. His father died when he was small. He and his sister were raised by their mother in a single parent household. He began piano lessons as a pre-schooler and never tired of the instrument. Sam loved his church and the whole family was very active in its busy schedule. It was only natural that he turned his talents toward the organ. When he was fifteen, Sam became the regular organist for his large Southern Baptist church.

Sam decided he wanted to be a nurse. He entered nursing school. Before he completed the program, Sam lost his desire for nursing, took a shorter course in respiratory technology, and headed into the job market.

Playing the organ was a joy, but there was one thing that troubled his relationship to the church. Sam, by the time he entered high school, knew that he was gay. Being the sensitive young man he was, he cowered and cringed at the ringing denunciations of homosexuals that he heard from the church's pulpit. He was never sexually active during high school and his vocational training. While completing his course in respiratory technology, he met a gay classmate. They became close friends but were never lovers. They were both deeply religious and decided that to be both religious and gay, they had to leave home territory. On a lark they decided to move to Anchorage, Alaska.

Both Sam and his friend found employment at Providence Hospital in Anchorage. They looked up the local Metropolitan Community Church. They were disappointed. The church was in turmoil. There was disagreement about how politically active the church should be in gay and feminist issues. Sam played the organ for a short time but decided he wanted to hear more Gospel and less gay activism. He dropped out.

Working at the hospital did not turn out to be the kind of challenge for which Sam was looking. He filled out an application at the post office, took the required tests, and was surprised at how quickly he was hired. Sam liked the post office. He enjoyed the people with whom he worked and enjoyed his contacts with customers. His life became even better when he was introduced to Mike, a gay civil engineer. They moved in together and began their life as mates.

I invited Sam to visit the church I pastored. He came and loved what he found. He liked the preaching. He loved the congregational singing and the songs they sang. And the church had purchased a new organ. Sam soon became the choir accompanist and eventually became the church choir director. He participated in many church functions, but always as a single person. Mike came to services only on rare occasions, usually when the choir was giving some special presentation. He would come to the service slightly late and leave before the last words of the benediction were said. While Sam felt accepted as an individual, he never believed he and Mike would be accepted as a couple. He was probably correct.

Sam's mother became seriously ill. Sam applied for a transfer back to Florida with the postal service. It was quickly approved. Mike followed. Together Sam and Mike attend a large Metropolitan Community Church. Sam has become the church organist.

TIM

Gay men and lesbians who have been raised in American Baptist families, churches, and parsonages are very special to me. As a lifelong American Baptist, I feel I have an even larger responsibility to them than to any other homosexuals. Tim is the son of an American Baptist minister. He grew up in American Baptist parsonages across the Midwest. He is a graduate of an American Baptist-related college. He received his law degree from Harvard. He is a junior partner in a large Anchorage law firm. To the public Tim is tightly closeted.

Tim is active in the community, serving on the boards of non-profit organizations, participating in a service club and the Anchorage Chamber of Commerce, and attending an Episcopal Church. He plays tennis at a highly competitive level. He dates women as a further cover of his sexual identity.

When I met Tim he very quickly shared his American Baptist heritage. He also shared that he was gay. (I had met him through a mutual gay friend.) He was living with another professional person with interests similar to his. I asked him how he related to his parents. They were completely unaware of his sexual orientation. He was their bachelor son, who they hoped would someday marry. I could understand why he had chosen to be closeted in Anchorage, but I questioned why he should perpetuate the dishonesty with his parents.

Tim decided to out himself to his parents on his next visit. After dinner one evening Tim decided it was the right time. He told them he was gay and that he was in a committed relationship with a lover in Anchorage. He explained that he had known he was gay since junior high. He explained further that his gayness was not a result of anything that either of his parents had done. They listened in stunned silence. Tim was not prepared for his father's reply, "If what you are saying is not a joke of some kind, you are no son of mine." Tim responded, "Then you are not my parents."

Tim did not bother to gather up his belongings. He rose from the table, walked to the door, and entered the dark of the night. He was headed back to Alaska. When he was about two blocks from his parent's home, he heard his father's voice yelling with full force. "Tim, Tim!" His father was running as he yelled. When he reached Tim, he grabbed him, hugged him, and then pulled him down to a seat on the curb along side of him. Tim's father exclaimed, "Nothing else matters. You are my son." Tim said it seemed as if they cried and hugged for almost an eternity.

Tim and his partner now visit Tim's parents together.

They feel genuinely welcomed and accepted. They share a bedroom when they visit. Tim's father still has not found the courage to share the family secret with his church, close friends, or fellow clergy.

URSULA

Ursula is a prototype of one of the emerging patterns among lesbians. The fact that she is the daughter of an accepting and encouraging Methodist minister has made it easier for her to be a pioneer. Ursula was clear in her mind that she was lesbian by the time she was a sophomore in high school She had a rock solid relationship with her parents. She talked with them. They let her know it was all right to be who she was.

When she became a student at a state university in Michigan, Ursula helped organize a campus organization of gays and lesbians. She marched and protested whenever injustice appeared and was a key promoter of gay and lesbian social events. After receiving her Bachelor's degree, she immediately pursued a Master's program in social work. Ursula met Pat during her Master's work. Pat was a graduate student in business administration. They fell in love, made promises to each other, and moved to Alaska following graduation.

Ursula is a social worker for one of the Anchorage hospitals. Pat decided that she wanted to be a CPA. She took additional training, passed her exam, and is now working for an accounting firm in Anchorage. Together they have income in excess of $100,000 per year. They have purchased a home in a nice neighborhood of Anchorage. They have adopted two children, both infants, who are of Alaskan Eskimo heritage. They are talking about one or the other of them becoming pregnant by artificial insemination. They enjoy parenting. They both identify themselves as Christians but are not church-involved. They do not know of a church that would accept them as the family they are. They do not want to be part of a "gay" church.

Both Ursula and Pat have strong feelings about gay and lesbian issues, but Ursula is the activist. I first met Ursula through her work as a social worker, but later worked with her as a fellow board member of Identity, Inc. She eventually became president of the organization. She is also active in the Committee for Equality, a non-profit organization formed to "advocate and secure full social and legal rights for gays, lesbians, and bisexual persons in Alaska." The organization is headed by an equally talented and committed lesbian who is the daughter of a prominent Episcopal priest.

Ursula and her family embody one of the waves of the future for women who are lesbian. To be associated with her is a delight.

VIC

Vic was the ideal kid as he grew up. He had an older brother and a younger sister. His brother looked after him, and his sister looked up to him. He was an excellent student in grade school. He was helpful to his parents, his teachers, and anyone else who was around. His attitude was "How can I be of help?" He was always the most popular kid in his class. The popularity extended through high school and into his adult life. How could anyone not like Vic?

Vic's mother noticed he began shutting the door of his room and spending much more time alone, almost always with his radio volume turned up high. Vic was eleven. His mother at first made nothing of it. Vic was starting through puberty. She reasoned that that was what it was all about. Eventually she started to be a bit concerned. One day while Vic was at school, she took a careful look at his room. She knew of no explanation for some of the things she found: trinkets, clothes, stamps, candy, items for personal hygiene. When Vic came home, she discreetly asked him where he was getting all the unexplained items. With much anguish he confessed that he had been stealing. His mother brought Vic's dad into the discussion. They decided that return of the items and payment out of his allowance for items that could not be returned would be sufficient discipline for his actions. Vic's parents made arrangements for him to see a counselor. He saw the counselor several times, and the incident seemed resolved.

What was never shared at that time was that Vic had already realized that he was sexually different. At the same time he was being loved by everyone, he hated himself. In the thefts, Vic was probably looking for punishment. All he got was acceptance and understanding. Vic never told the counselor about his developing dilemma, and the counselor never guessed.

Vic is as handsome as he is personable. He found a home in the drama department of his high school. He acted, he sang, and he danced. The girls loved him. He dated often but dated no one with regularity. He was chosen "most likely to succeed" by his high school graduating class.

In college Vic kept pursuing the theater. He also became sexually active with someone of the same sex for the first time. After two years of college theater, he moved to New York to try his hand at professional theater. He waited tables, took all kinds of lessons, went to countless auditions, and went nowhere. He had become another starving actor. Out of economic necessity Vic applied for a sales rep job with a cosmetics company. The job required a lot of travel and allowed him to live wherever he wanted on the East Coast. For unknown reasons Vic was a Baltimore Orioles fan as a boy. He moved to Baltimore and made it his hometown. There he met an architect who grew up in Alaska.

Vic and his partner are active members of a large Presbyterian church. Vic sings in the choir. They have established excellent relationships with their families in Alaska and California. They visit their families and family members visit them. They watch a lot of Oriole games and love the cultural advantages of the Baltimore-Washington DC area. They serve as Big Brothers to two Baltimore children.

WANDA

If I did not know her, I would not believe this outrageously wonderful person existed.   She combines a foulmouthed "to hell with you" attitude with genuine caring and a smile on her face. Wanda is now a senior citizen nearing her seventieth birthday. She loves her six cats, but I cannot repeat her evaluation of the presidency of George Bush.

Wanda was born with a silver spoon in her mouth. Her father made money while others lost money during the Great Depression. The family was as Catholic as they were wealthy. Wanda was supposed to be a boy, but that was one thing her father was not able to control. She was not only not a boy, she was no ordinary girl. She was lesbian. The nuns kept her under control during her Catholic grade school years, but neither of the Catholic boarding schools she attended could. She was kicked out of both for her not-too-hidden sexual activities. She finally graduated from public high school as a smoking, drinking, foulmouthed eighteen-year-old who had told the Catholic Church to go to hell.

Wanda's next step was the University of Oklahoma where she earned a degree in mechanical engineering. World War II was about to end when she enlisted in the Women's Army Corps and was commissioned a Second Lieutenant. By the end of her four-year commitment, Wanda knew her place was definitely not in the Army. She worked for a variety of engineering firms, but could never see herself being promoted or being given responsibility with the same consideration as her male counterparts. She heard there was opportunity in Alaska. She has now been in Alaska for thirty years.

Wanda's years in Alaska have been full. She worked for the City of Anchorage for twenty-five years. She met Shirley, and they were together for twenty-two years before Shirley died of cancer. Wanda helped organize the first lesbian groups in Anchorage. She gave encouragement and counsel to dozens of younger women as they sorted out their sexuality and lifestyles. She has lots of friends. She really did not care when she heard her father disowned her before he died.

One day Wanda gave one of her tirades against religion to a lesbian friend of mine. My friend responded that not all ministers and churches were like those she so despised. She challenged Wanda to go with her to a service in the church I then pastored.

Communion was being celebrated in the service that Wanda and my friend attended. Before the celebration I extended the invitation to participate, observing, "There are no strangers at the Lord's table." For the first time in almost fifty years Wanda received communion. She wept. Wanda is now one of my treasured friends.

XAVIER

Xavier is an Hispanic son of immigrant parents. The family had broken from its Catholic heritage and kept no formal religious ties. An American Baptist church was in their neighborhood, and one summer Xavier was recruited to attend Vacation Bible School. He loved the teachers, the church, and the other kids. He was hooked. At the end of VBS the church gave him a new Bible. It became his treasure.

Spiritual things were natural for Xavier. He found talking to God quite natural. He also believed God talked to him. By the time he was twelve, he knew that God was calling him to be a minister. The pastor of the church became his role model. As he went through high school and college at a state university in the area, he never doubted that God had called him to the ministry.

Xavier's great conflict was that he was sure he was called to be a minister, but he was just as sure that he was homosexual. He handled the problem by being celibate. After college came seminary training. He loved seminary as much as he loved that first Vacation Bible School. He had many friends, both male and female. He was very social and popular. He remained celibate and never dated.

During seminary Xavier worked with youth in an all-white, primarily middle- and upper-class church. The fact that he was Hispanic made no difference to the church. The youth group flourished. The budding young minister was asked to preach from time to time and always did a commendable job. As graduation neared, the church decided to call Xavier as their assistant minister. They recommended him for ordination.

I was part of the council that examined Xavier for ordination. He presented an excellent ordination paper. During the questioning about his call to the ministry and theological beliefs, he was articulate and confident. Then came about a quarter hour of tension. Two of the panel members hit upon the fact that he was not married. They asked if he had plans to marry. He was asked if he dated. He was asked about his childhood. He was asked if anything unusual happened to him during his childhood. Xavier and almost everyone else knew what they were after. He was relieved that they never asked the obvious unspoken question, "Are you a homosexual?"

Xavier was ordained and served the church for six years as its assistant minister. His bachelorhood was a common joke around the church. Someone was always trying to fix him up with the ideal woman. Xavier decided it was time to move on and placed his name in the personnel system of the

127

denomination in search for a pastorate. Apparently churches were skittish about calling an unmarried minister. He was offered a job in a denominational office. He took the job.

Xavier remains celibate. He has discreetly made himself known to open gays and lesbians in the denomination. He would like to speak out, but it would probably mean the end of his employment. At times he is enraged because of the prejudice that he feels has kept him from fulfilling the completeness of his calling to the ministry.

YVES

Yves often wished he could have been a Bill, a Joe, or a Hank. Being an Yves was not as easy as he would have preferred. The only other Eves he knew were female. He knew he was male. He knew he wasn't female. But in other ways as he was growing up, he really couldn't figure out what he was. From the time Yves could remember he preferred doing things that girls usually do. He loved to help his mother with household chores. He liked to cook. His mother was an excellent seamstress, and Yves wanted to learn that skill in the worst way. His father, a jock in his younger days, wanted his son to be an athlete. Yves wanted no part of athletic competition. Before junior high years, Yves developed mannerisms that were readily identified as effeminate. By age nine he knew he was somehow different from other boys. By age twelve he had heard about fags and knew he was growing up to be one.

The theater department of his junior high was the place Yves found acceptance. He sang well, danced well, and was a good natural clown when around friendly folks. While never a star, Yves almost always got a part in every production, and when he did not, he was the first to volunteer to serve on the stage crew. His junior high experience continued into high school. He loved the applause of the audience.

128

A group of high school bullies, all of whom happened to play on the football team, decided it was their responsibility to take care of the fags of the school. Yves fit their stereotype. He was a sophomore when it happened. One evening following a rehearsal, he was walking home when a carload of the predators pulled alongside and began taunting him. He began running. They sped ahead. Three jumped out of the car, grabbed him, and pulled him into the vehicle. Yves was taken to a park where he was forced to participate in acts of sodomy. He did not resist, believing his safety and even his life was in jeopardy. He was warned of the dire consequences of telling anyone. He knew all of the teenage thugs by name. He saw them daily at school. They would smirk as they passed him by. It was five years before he could share his experience of terror.

Several of the youth from the church I pastored were active in the performing arts department of the high school. They invited Yves to be a part of the group, and he gladly accepted. He found another safe place in the church youth group. He made one more religious detour. He heard of the marvelous things that were happening at the local Assembly of God. There were reports of healings and transformations. For a few weeks Yves believed he had been delivered of his homosexual feelings. It was a cruel interlude. The feelings came back.

Yves's other move to safety was dating. After his rape experience he was hardly ever without a date. When a fellow male high school student, who turned out to be gay, flirted with Yves, he turned him away with the comment, "I have a girl friend." He was terrified by the thought that someone might in fact know he was gay.

Following high school graduation, Yves got a job as a bank teller. He also continued his education part-time at the local community college. While playing a minor role in a musical production of the college, Yves met Larry. They became a couple. They rented an apartment together. In the new relationship Yves at last felt comfortable being the person he was. He became an excellent tailor and a marvelous cook. More recently he has become manager of an upscale women's clothing store.

ZACHARY

Zach is a ministerial colleague. He is the pastor of a Metropolitan Community Church. I met him at a continuing education seminar for ministers. Those attending the seminar represented a wide range of denominational traditions. Even though Metropolitan Community Churches are less than welcome in most ecumenical circles, I was pleased to see how welcome he seemed to be at this particular seminar. At the seminar a friendship was initiated. We continue to keep in contact with each other. I was curious about Zach's spiritual journey that had led to ordination and service in the Universal Fellowship of Metropolitan Community Churches. This is his story:

Zach was destined to be religious. He was raised in a devout Roman Catholic family. His education was parochial from beginning to end. He attended Catholic grade school, high school, and then began college in a seminary as he looked forward to the Catholic priesthood. He loved God, the Church, and the worship life of the Church. Being an altar boy was a thrill. His parents were pleased, and they looked forward with great pride at the possibility of having a son who was a priest of the Church.

By the time Zach was in first grade, he knew he had a strong drive other than religion. He had a special attraction to other boys. By age fifteen he had found a teenage boyfriend. They liked each other very much and spent as much time together as they could. Neither was effeminate in appearance and so their friendship was not looked upon with suspicion. Their dates were often for a movie at the local drive-in theater. They could make out in the cozy privacy of his friend's car. There was no doubt they were both gay, but they kept the real nature of their relationship tightly closeted.

The guilt was terrible. Zach couldn't reconcile his sexual interests and the practice of his faith. He went to confession with regularity. He confessed masturbation but nothing more. Eventually the guilt was more than he could handle. He dropped out of seminary and moved to California. In San Francisco, Zach met Wally. Wally was just as religious and just as Catholic as was Zach. They became a couple. Troy Perry, founder of the Metropolitan Community Churches, was much talked about in San Francisco. Zach and Wally, knowing they would never have Catholic blessing in their relationship, decided to contact Troy Perry in Los Angeles. They made a trip to Los Angeles, completed the required counseling, and their relationship was blessed as a Holy Union.

Zach and Wally felt good about their relationship but could not yet leave the Catholic Church. They attended mass regularly and participated in confession. Zach still wanted to be a priest. Eventually he accepted that as a gay man with a commitment to his partner for life, Catholic ordination would never happen. He gave up the idea of being a priest in the Catholic Church and revised his goal to ordination in the Metropolitan Community Church. Under the supervision of the church, he began to study for ordination. With his Catholic educational background, his training through the MCC, and his commitment to continuing education through seminars and a personal reading program, Zach has become a knowledgeable and articulate minister of the gospel in the MCC. He admits that he is a bit high church in his leading of worship.

Even after his ordination in the MCC, when Zach went back to visit his parents in New Jersey, he attended mass with

131

them and received communion. About four years ago on a visit with his parents, he was refused communion because he failed to go to confession. Zach decided it was time to make the final break with the Catholic church. He hasn't attended a Catholic mass since.

As a pastor of an MCC congregation, a very sizable part of his time is given to ministry with victims of AIDS. He is quite certain he did not misunderstand his calling to be a minister and a priest of God.

Chapter 5

PERSONAL INTRODUCTION, A REVIEW

A scientifically accurate summary statement about the make up of the gay and lesbian population is impossible. The body of research on the homosexual population is continually growing. Every piece of research is welcome and helpful. However, results of all gay-lesbian research are flawed, and the applications of the research are limited accordingly. In Chapter 2 of Part II, I have already mentioned two research projects. The most massive of those projects is the Kinsey Institute's research on homosexualities, published in 1978 and authored by Bell and Weinberg. The second is Identity, Inc.'s research project on the gay and lesbian population in Alaska.

The limitations of the Kinsey report are enormous. The distortions were inevitable because of the area (San Francisco) chosen to recruit a pool of respondents. The study is further compromised by the sources used to recruit respondents. For the study the primary sources of respondents were gay bars, homophile print media of the San Francisco area, bath houses, and homophile organizations. Since San Francisco has become a major gathering point for gay openness and activism, the city does not have a gay and lesbian population that is typical of the overall population of the nation. The gay population in other places is far more hidden. Further, the particular sources used for recruitment reflect lifestyles that are not even typical of the San Francisco area, let alone the nation. The report is an accurate study of the particular homosexual individuals who participated in the study. Its results cannot be projected onto the general population.

The same limitations are found with the Identity study of

Alaskan homosexuals. Identity acknowledges these limitations in the introduction of its report. It states: "The inherent limitations in any research with this population is that most gays and lesbians conceal their orientation from others to a high degree . . . a truly random sampling is nearly impossible to achieve."[22] Identity used the existing networks to recruit respondents. Inevitably this resulted in heavy use of the Anchorage gay bars for distribution of questionnaires.

With this method and use of gay bars, it is not surprising that over one-third of all respondents identified themselves as potential problem drinkers. Even though gay bars are very important to the social structure of a part of the homosexual population, the bars would never produce an acceptable sampling for any study of homosexuals that might be used to make projections about the entire homosexual population and their drinking and drug use patterns.

Religion is another subject about which Identity's report can never be used for generalizations. Identity's report found that 57 percent of their respondents no longer participate in any religious tradition. It is perfectly proper to ask what would happen to that figure had Identity's sampling touched the very sizable closeted homosexual population in the churches.

It is inescapable to conclude that while studies of the homosexual populations are helpful, they are always limited in value by the pool of respondents that can be recruited to participate. Gay men and lesbians have developed astounding abilities to hide. Having developed those abilities, they do not suddenly forget them when a researcher approaches them with questions about their sexuality. The more typical homosexual persons will be hesitant to participate in surveys and would possibly not tell the truth if they did participate.

Recognizing these limitations in research, can we ever know how many gay men and lesbians are among us? Probably not. But we have no shortage of estimates. When I first began my journey of awareness of homosexuals, I heard and read figures that ranged from 2 to 8 percent. Today the most popular figure is 10 percent. I have never seen or heard of any study that establishes 10 percent or any other figure.

Alfred Kinsey's *Sexual Behavior in the Human Male*[23] was published in 1948 and his *Sexual Behavior in the Human Female*[24] was published in 1953. Both of these studies attempted to establish some percentage figures on the homosexual presence. However, Kinsey's very artificial 0-6 scale produced a blending effect between homosexuality and heterosexuality that leaves us with something less than precise figures.

The homosexual minority is the most difficult of all minorities to study. Other minorities are based on race, religion, economics, age, occupation, language, or some other distinguishing feature that is relatively easy to isolate and study. I have heard statements such as "Thirty percent of all alcoholics are homosexuals." "Nineteen percent of the American economy is controlled by homosexuals." "Thirty percent of all teenage suicides are homosexuals." "The average homosexual has sexual contacts with as many as thirty different people per year." The quotes go on and on. Once they are uttered, they are repeated and repeated again. They are repeated on television, reported in national magazines, and echoed in Sunday sermons. But I have never found any justifying research for any of these percentage quotes.

Homosexual persons cannot be identified except by themselves. They have found by hard experience that when they do identify themselves as gay or lesbian, bad things happen. They remain hidden and unresponsive to all kinds of sociological research.

With these realities, how can we ever construct a valid picture of the homosexual population for those who have avoided the subject? While I have read widely on the subject for over twenty years and am aware of much of the research that continues to be done, I am just one more person with limited, distorted, and incomplete information.   It is against this background that I decided to build a profile of the homosexual population from anecdotal reports, not research as such. The 26 gay and lesbian persons I have described in the previous chapter represent people I have known.   I chose and constructed the short biographies with a conscious attempt to make them typical of the homosexual population I personally know.   I am sure they are not typical of the general homosexual population.

Building a profile of the homosexual population on anecdotal information has significant weaknesses. It also has at least two significant strengths. First, it provides a "feel" for the diversity of the population. Anecdotal research communicates living realities that are usually not conveyed in cold statistics, no matter how accurate the statistics might be.   Second, this particular anecdotally based summary may well match quite well the gay and lesbian population which ministers and churches will most likely encounter.   Just as the scientifically conducted sociological studies are both helpful and limited, so also will the following summary statements have limitations but also genuine value.

The summary I offer is not quantitative.   Rather it is descriptive of the population I know.

HIDDENNESS

The makeup of the gay and lesbian population cannot be understood apart from their loneliness and developed ability to hide. Identity's study found that their respondents were aware of their same-sex orientation for an average of eight years before sharing this information with another human being. I have never known a gay or lesbian person who has not gone through this extended period of loneliness and hiding. These years of silence inevitably shape the patterns of living for all the rest of their lives.

Imagine the dilemma and frustration of the gay teenager. He becomes aware of his sexual attraction to other boys. All of the other boys are talking about girls. He has no sexual interest in girls. Social life beginning with junior high revolves around girl and boy relationships. Everybody wants to know whom he likes. For a gay teenager to answer that question honestly, for instance, "I like John," would be a disaster. There is enormous pressure for conformity during these years, and an honest answer would establish our gay teenager as the worst type of non-conformist. So for the sake of social acceptance, the young gay boy tells a lie. "I like Susie." When the big school dance comes he asks Susie to go with him, He may enjoy dancing, but as he dances with Susie, he is aware that he would really like the experience of dancing with John. He would like to touch the one he really likes.

Meanwhile, he is expected to take required sex education classes. Everything that is said in the class fails to match up with his own feelings and desires. In this setting and in others with the same dynamics, he learns not only that he is different, he begins to conclude that something is wrong with him. It is confirmed that a male and female express themselves sexually to each other by the male placing his penis inside the female's vagina. Our young teenager, with no help from any source, wonders how two males might sexually express themselves to each other.

Typically the gay teenager is aware of what he feels before having any idea what to call it. He hears words like queer, fag, fairy, fruit, and eventually, homosexual and gay. The first years of his same-sex awareness are a horror of loneliness and hiding. Since homosexuality is not a subject of discussion at home, at church, or among his friends, our young gay man begins believing that he may be the only person in the whole world who has this set of feelings. Eventually he concludes that there are others who have these feelings, but he has no idea who they are. He is terrified with the thought of making himself known to someone he suspects is gay and being wrong. By the time he is a junior or senior in high school, he becomes aware of the macho gangs who regularly go out hunting for queers to beat up.

The lying that began with "I like Susie" becomes a pattern of living. The young gay dates girls as a cover of his true sexuality. Girls may experience him as fun, gentlemanly, kind, generous, and sexually respectful. The whole exercise becomes a cruel hoax, a well-planned lie that is perceived as being necessary for survival.

At our teenager's church, he finds no help. He finds either silence or condemnation. He is told that his same-sex desires are a matter of his own choice. He knows different. He knows that he would quickly and gladly choose to be heterosexual, if that option were available. He has tried a variety of ways to become heterosexual and nothing has worked. If our teenager happens to be Catholic, there is the possibility of celibacy. Many Catholic gay young people start the process of becoming a priest. As studies now show, the result is a Catholic priesthood that is heavily gay.[25]

No matter how deeply the gay teenager desires to be religious, to be religious in an institutional setting means he must lie to someone, either to himself or to his church. The deep sense of guilt that pervades his spiritual life takes over his whole being. He finds guilt and loneliness to be a deadening and deadly combination.

At home another kind of torture develops. Mother and father have hopes, dreams, and aspirations for their son. None of their desires for their son are for him to be homosexual. Parents look forward to their son's wedding and the claiming of a daughter-in-law. They look forward to grandchildren. They participate in the "Who do you like?" game from grade school years on. Parents encourage dating. They want to meet their son's girlfriends. They have no idea their son has no interest in their game. Our gay teenager merely finds one more arena in which he must lie to maintain acceptance, one more arena in which he plays the cruel game of hiding in order to survive.

The teenage gay is fully justified in his fears. I have never known a single parent who responded with happiness when a son revealed his homosexuality. Many parents respond with genuine acceptance and understanding, but never joy. They are never eager to share with others that their son is gay. They are embarrassed by their son's partner or lover. In their inept responses they only add to their son's loneliness. They hope their son moves away. He usually does.

Much has been made of the loneliness of our present age. It is rather easy to understand how it has happened. Mobility of our population, increased reliance on impersonal forms of communication (radio, TV, computers), the social acceptance of divorce, and reliance on professional people in the solving of personal problems are just some of the factors which contribute to our national loneliness. But in the discussion of loneliness, I have never once heard anyone mention the loneliness produced by the growing-up experience of the gay man. Gay loneliness is truly profound. The aloneness is the correctly perceived need, for the sake of safety, to hide. The hidden loneliness is the key to understanding both gay strengths and urgent needs.

The lesbian population experiences most of the same dynamics, but there are significant differences. Close, even affectionate, relationships between women are socially acceptable. Girls can hold hands in public. They can embrace. At a high school dance, they can dance together. They can go to the home of a girl friend, stay overnight and sleep in the same bed, and no questions are raised. There are no female goon squads waiting to accost female couples. (Lesbians are much more apt to be raped by a male than to be attacked by gangs of females.)   Girls come to an awareness of their same-sex preferences at an older age than gay boys. They are slower to acknowledge their sexual preference to another person. They are more apt to hold out the hope that they will respond positively to heterosexual relationships in a marriage.

During the years of her sexual secrecy, the teenage lesbian experiences the same conflict between her own sexual feelings and public norms as do her male counterparts. They find no source of help. Homosexuality is either a never-discussed subject, or a subject of rejection, ridicule, and condemnation. Family, church, school, and peers all contribute. Guilt, low self-esteem, game playing, denying, and loneliness are all the inevitable consequences.

The easiest solution for the lesbian is a heterosexual marriage. Prior to the women's liberation movement, it was almost her only option. It was and still is an attractive hope since lesbians desire children no less than heterosexual women. Once in a heterosexual marriage, many, many lesbians find reasons to stay in that relationship. Children are born. Wife and children become economically dependent on a husband. Accommodations are made. And divorces occur. Even then, motherhood and divorce provide hiding places. Whether a lesbian never marries, or if she marries and stays in what becomes a peculiar marriage, or if she divorces and seeks a new family pattern, she—as does a gay man—needs to hide from family, employer, church, and neighbor. She is probably even more hidden to the general public than is her male counterpart. She has learned by experience that her survival depends on successfully hiding. She hides and does it very effectively.

ANGER

Homosexuals are angry, and they have every right to be. As a Christian pastor, I have had to come to terms with God's anger as portrayed in the Scriptures, my own anger, and the anger of others, especially when it is turned on me or on some innocent bystander.

Our capacity for anger is God-given, and that anger is to be treasured. Anger is to be respected, trained, and disciplined. Anger properly used is not an enemy of love, but an ally. Anger is the natural surge of energy that occurs when a human being is confronted with injustice. Anger is as natural as eating and sleeping. Without it we would be defenseless from attack, injustice would never be challenged, and the path of sin and evil would never be blocked.

The Bible indicates God does not hesitate to be identified with anger. God restrains his anger (Psalm 78:38), directs his anger (Isaiah 10:25), defers his anger (Isaiah 48:9), turns his anger (Jeremiah 2:35), and slows his anger (Psalm 15:8). We human beings have abused God's creation. We should not be surprised that we have angered the creator. The disciplining of his anger is a part of God's grace toward us all.

We humankind have been created in our God's image. The capacity for anger came in the package. We cause problems with our anger when we fail to discipline it. When we fail to discipline our anger, we bring about destruction rather than the needed change. We all need to develop the ability to restrain, direct, defer, turn, and slow the enormous energy generated by injustice.

When I describe the homosexual population as extraordinarily angry, I mean no criticism. The injustices done to them ought to call forth an abundance of anger.

Consider the dynamic. Gay and lesbian persons are condemned, criticized, penalized, abused, and rejected for something inherent in their makeup, which they did not cause nor choose. Because of societal training they first experience their sexuality not as a gift but as an injustice The injustice is not short-termed. As they experience their sexuality, it is

141

perceived as a cruel life sentence. Understandably God the creator becomes the object of their anger. When in anger homosexual persons shake their fists at God and cry out, "Why did you make me thus?" it is understandable. It is existential anger that cries out of their very being. Paul dismisses people who make this cry to God (Romans 9). According to Paul, God has a right to make vessels of dishonor. That is not good news to gay and lesbian persons who are struggling to find meaning in a developing painful life.

Young gay and lesbian persons start processing their anger while they are still in their extended period of loneliness. Blaming oneself is all too easy. Anger is often turned inward. Out of anger turned inward, gays and lesbians consider suicide in distressing numbers. Eventually the anger is expressed against government that denies them equal protection, organizations and businesses that discriminate against them, and parents who reject them. Homosexuals are very angry. Like the rest of us, they might not use their anger appropriately, but the intense anger that is there is fully justified.

STRESS

The life of the gay population is full of stress. If the struggle for self acceptance were not enough, consider the struggle to find some level of acceptance in the world in which they live. "Coming out" is the process of disclosing one's sexual orientation to another person. Gay men and lesbians think long and hard before revealing their sexual orientation to anyone. The fear of rejection, discrimination, and condemnation is a well-founded fear.

Coming out is not a one-time experience. It is a lifelong process that is never completed. Into every new situation and relationship, the question is presented anew. Should I out myself to this person? If I do, what will be the consequences?

Every gay and lesbian person lives with the reality that a

line must be drawn somewhere. Consequences are waiting no matter where the line of openness is drawn. Few people in the general population live under equivalent stress. At stake are family relationships, church relationships. employment security, business opportunity, political viability, choice of residence, and personal safety.

To complicate the predicament even more, there are few opportunities for the release of the stress. Today more gay and lesbian social opportunities are being created, but the process is slow. There are no gay Rotary or Kiwanis clubs. Gay military veterans are not free to be themselves at the local American Legion or VFW. Very few churches are safe havens. Mental health providers and self-help groups are seen as too risky for full disclosure. The most available opportunities for gay social life are found in gay bars. Gay bars are found in almost every city in America with a population over 100 thousand. They are very successful, but they also present a dilemma. The combination of stress and alcohol is producing alcohol abuse of tragic proportions. Homosexuals believe they are more vulnerable to alcoholism than any other group in our society.

Gay churches are still in their infancy, but they hold a great potential as a gathering of openly gay and lesbian persons in which the stress of everyday life can be escaped.

Society offers no helping hand. Gays and lesbians are left in their stressed-out condition.

DIVERSITY

Homosexuals are typically dismissed as a category as though there were no variety among them. In reality homosexuals are as diverse as the general population.

The homosexual population is diverse in appearance. Certainly there are a handful of gay men who are effeminate in appearance. There are some lesbians who fit the butch image. Of the 26 persons I described in Chapter 4, no more than four or five could be described as effeminate or butch. I have known heterosexual men and women who fit the public stereotype as well as any of the four or five homosexuals I have described. Add the reality that most gay men and lesbians intentionally dress and act to be hidden in the general population, and we find that by nature and by intentional act, homosexuals are very diverse in appearance.

The homosexual population is diverse in its employment. Some industries are more accepting of gay men and lesbians than others. Some of these are the floral industry, restaurants, the entertainment industry, retailers of most kinds, the beauty industry, and the fashion industry. Large concentrations of gay and lesbian workers are found in all these industries. Most professions are tolerant of homosexuals, based on competence and low-profile behavior. The ranks of medical doctors, lawyers, dentists, teachers, social workers, and therapists of many kinds are being swelled by homosexuals who are willing to remain closeted to some degree. Government is a typically benign employer of gay men and lesbians. Homosexuals abound in the post office, health and human services departments, insurance and finance departments, regulatory agencies, libraries, and most other governmental offices. Another group of homosexuals have pursued careers in surroundings that require them to be publicly closeted and privately discreet. A surprising number of homosexuals who play the hiding game with skill find careers in police and fire departments, professional sports, and elected offices.

Two employers remain openly hostile to gay men and lesbians: churches and the military. Even in the military many homosexuals discipline themselves and survive the hostile environment. In Identity's *One in Ten* study, 31 percent of all male respondents were veterans of the U.S. military. A few are gaining acceptance as ministers, usually in special circumstances. Churches remain the toughest of all job markets for gay men and lesbians.

The homosexual population is diverse in sexual lifestyle. Whenever the term "the gay lifestyle" is used, it is a reference to an assumed pattern of sexual behavior. It is an unfair characterization, a stereotyping of all gay men. "The gay lifestyle" is an indication of ignorance on the part of the person using the term. The image that lies behind the term includes sexual orgies, bath houses, prostitution, gay bars as pick-up points, cruising, and promiscuity in general.

Just as there are heterosexuals who misuse their sexuality through perversion, prostitution, and promiscuity; so also there are some homosexuals who have abused and misused their sexuality. But this represents only a small portion of the homosexual population among us. More typically the homosexual's need to hide has created life patterns that are disciplined rather than *laissez faire*. I believe that is true in their sexual practices as well as other areas of their lives.

Gay and lesbian teenagers are far less sexually active than their heterosexual counterparts. This reflects the fact that they are still closeted during their teen years. Even as the gay young man begins to emerge out of the closet, he is very cautious. Today once out of the closet the young gay man finds himself under the influence of the dire threat of AIDS. This dynamic has made the gay population increasingly responsible in their sexuality. The growing norm among homosexuals is the practice of sexuality in the context of a committed, long-term relationship. The typical gay or lesbian person whom I know is looking for a committed, monogamous partnership. "The gay lifestyle" is foreign to them. An urgent need among young gay men and lesbians is guidance and instruction about finding such partnerships and about what a responsible homosexual sex life means.

The homosexual population is diverse in its location. Not all homosexuals are rushing to San Francisco, Greenwich, or Key

West. While cities have provided an easier environment in which to hide, the bulk of the gay and lesbian population has chosen to remain scattered in cities and towns of every size. In Alaska, Anchorage, the state's largest city, is a gathering point for homosexuals. However, they are also found in every city, village, and community of the state. I have been thoroughly and pleasantly surprised at the number of gay men and lesbians I have met here in the Matanuska Valley. Homosexuals may move 3,000 miles away from their hometown, but the hometown they seek out is very diverse.

Homosexuals are also diverse in the ways they are housed. They live in apartments, condominiums, and increasingly in homes which they have purchased. In the Identity *One in Ten* study, 41 percent of all respondents lived in a home they owned. Homosexuals live in almost every neighborhood. They may well be your next door neighbor.

CREATIVITY

Are homosexuals more creative than the general population? I believe they are. I have no studies; I have no statistics to offer as proof. My belief is based on my knowledge, my personal experiences, and my observations of artistic, performing, and literary circles. Gay and lesbian actors, musicians, dancers, singers, artists, writers, directors, poets, and choreographers abound. I have asked myself "Why?" Allow me a speculation.

The dynamics of loneliness, anger, fear, and stress form a roaring river that rushes over the soul of the homosexual. It is relentless and never ending. Someone has suggested that it is like the gushing, raging river that carved out the phenomenon we call the Grand Canyon. When visiting the Grand Canyon, I tried to imagine the waters that cut away the soils of present day Arizona. I also marveled at the beauty of the walls of the Canyon that were laid bare by the process.

The typical homosexual person has spent long years with the soul being torn asunder. They have experienced the tearing apart of their inner being. They have lived with deep wounds. They have taken long looks at the walls of their soul laid bare. Should I be surprised when my gay and lesbian friends present me with glimpses of life that I never otherwise could see?

Collectively the homosexual population has blessed our world with creative works that help us to understand and appreciate the Creator's work. We all owe them an enormous debt.

In summary, homosexuals are a mostly hidden, diverse, creative, angry, and stressed population. I can only pray that the heterosexual majority will take time to know their homosexual brothers and sisters. It has to be done one at a time and will take time. The sooner we start, the richer we all will be.

Chapter 6

THE CHURCH'S MINISTRY TO HOMOSEXUAL PERSONS

There is a great gulf between the Christian churches and the homosexual population. Prior to the Stonewall Inn incident, the churches lived in the bliss of silence and ignorance. The typical Christian knew nothing of the homosexual phenomenon and there was no pressure to learn. The social justice energy of the churches was still involved in the issues of racial justice and the Vietnam War. It was relatively easy to ignore the addition of one more explosive issue to the churches' agendas.

As gay liberation took hold and gay men and lesbians began coming out of the closet, Christians and churches, rather than becoming informed and responding with concern, went on the attack against homosexuals. The aggressive homosexual pioneers became a favorite target of preachers. Gay and lesbian Christians who came out of their closets were ostracized. The exiting process of homosexuals from the churches was a quiet venture and is continuing to this day.

Currently and concretely, the issue that is being used as a platform for debate in the churches is ordination of homosexuals. The issue of blessing gay and lesbian couples follows close behind. All major Protestant main line denominations have called for conversations and discussions. Everyone is nervous about starting any serious discussions in local churches.

It is correctly perceived that serious discussion will take Christians far beyond the issues of ordination and the blessing of same-sex couples. The fear is that even a discussion will open Pandora's box and will result in a significant exodus of heterosexuals from main line churches as they move to more conservative and less aggressive churches.

Since World War II Americans have developed a freedom to leave the churches of their childhood. In his March, 1992, commentary on religion and culture,[26] Martin Marty reports that in 1955 only 4 percent of the American adult population had left the faith of their childhood. By 1985, one-third had done so. Studies of the homosexual population show they are part of that exodus. They have massively left the faith of their childhood.

The exodus of homosexuals is different from the exodus of others because they have not left over issues of basic belief, creedal confession, or even indifference. They have not left for lack of love of their faith. They have left because they are victims of gross injustice. They have left, for the most part, quietly. Their exodus has a hiddenness consistent with their hidden sexual orientation. They have left with intense anger.

While a significant number of gay men and lesbians remain in the churches, they are very closeted. They participate in worship and partake of the sacraments, but the churches' ministry to them is limited by their closed closet doors. Homosexuals in the church are every bit as angry as those who have left.

Churches have already lost many of their most talented and sensitive people as homosexuals have left. A residual dilemma threatens any church that opens honest discussion on the forbidden subject. They will face the loss of many people who see no point in talking about homosexuals. Every church that seriously considers ministry with homosexuals will do so at significant cost.

According to the Scriptures, God has given particular ministries to churches. Foremost among those is the ministry of reconciliation. Paul lays out the church's ministry in II Corinthians:

> So if anyone is in Christ, there is a new creation.
> Everything old is passed away; see, everything has
> become new! All this is from God who reconciled us
> to himself through Christ, and has given us the ministry
> of reconciliation; that is, in Christ God was reconciling
> the world to himself, not counting their trespasses
> against them, and entrusting the message of
> reconciliation to us. (II Corinthians 5:17-19 NRSV)

The great gulf that now exists between homosexuals and the
churches is a very concrete challenge to the ministry of
reconciliation that God has given to churches.

I have already suggested that reconciliation and the
ministry can occur only when heterosexuals and homosexuals get
to know one another. Under the present circumstances it is
impossible to know one another. Even though we work together,
shop together, live in the same neighborhoods, and even go
through formal worship together, we cannot know one another.
This is the dynamic that must be broken.

Gay and lesbian persons are hidden, angry, and fearful.
On the other side, heterosexual Christians are uninformed,
misinformed, judgmental, and fearful. If we are to hope for a
successful meeting, we must start by getting our information
straight.

Basic, largely undisputed information about homosexuality
has been known for a good many years. In 1978, Abigail
VanBuren in her "Dear Abby" column gave her readers a true-
false test about homosexuality. Her questions were, at least in
part, designed to challenge superstitions and myths about being
gay. According to Abby, known facts in 1978 were as follows:

1. Homosexuals do NOT commit more crimes than
   heterosexuals.

2. People do NOT become gay because they have

151

been seduced by a gay man when young.

3. Homosexuals CANNOT be identified by the way they act, dress, and talk.

4. Men are NOT homosexual because they were raised by domineering mothers.

5. Many gay people CAN and DO become the biological parents of children.

6. Homosexuals are NOT more inclined to molest children than heterosexuals.

7. A few sexual experiences with someone of the same sex does NOT mean that a person is gay.

8. The American Psychiatric Association does NOT consider homosexuals to be "sick."

9. Homosexual couples CANNOT be legally married in the United States.

10. Most homosexuals do NOT try to convert young people into becoming gay.

11. Children raised by gay parents are NOT more likely to become homosexual themselves.

To Abby's list of eleven facts, three more should be added:

12. Homosexuals do NOT choose their sexual orientation.

13.   Same-sex orientation IS rooted in genetics.

14.   A person's orientation toward homosexuality
        CANNOT be changed.

The injustices against our homosexual brothers and sisters will never be corrected until we get these basic facts straight in our minds.   When heterosexual and homosexual meet face to face, the success of the meeting is unavoidably dependent on having the facts straight.   Incorrect information will inevitably destroy our ministry of reconciliation.   It is truth that sets us free. Untruth binds us and enslaves us all.

One more fact must be faced.   The churches have falsely accused and judged our homosexual brothers and sisters.   Our first sin is that we have judged at all.   We should know better. The Gospel of John records Jesus's claim to authority.   "The Father judges no one but has given all judgment to the son." (John 5:22 NRSV)   Matthew records Jesus's warning about the dire consequences of usurping that authority.   "Do not judge, so that you may not be judged, for with the judgment you make you will be judged." (Matthew 7:1,2 NRSV).

For us to judge anyone, even the guilty, is unacceptable to our Lord.   We have been grossly irresponsible by judging and condemning homosexuals for nothing that they have done.   We have inexcusably judged them for who they are.

If Christians and churches hope to establish a relationship of trust with gay men and lesbians, repentance, apology, and a plea for forgiveness must clear the way.   We church people need the forgiveness of God and the homosexual for the judgments we have made.

A third reality must be faced.   It is our fear.   There are positive functions for fear.   Without fear we would not know when danger is near.   It is the warning light, the caution light of life.   Sometimes fear can go awry.   Fear based on false information, rather than contributing to our security, betrays us.

Fears that go out of control become paralyzing. Fears that are undefined can become unattached anxieties that keep us from positive actions.

Fear of people we perceive to be unlike us is very common. The public perception of homosexuals is that they are more unlike the majority of the population than like them. It is believed there is something about "the homosexual lifestyle" that makes them almost totally different. The opposite is true. Accepting as fact that homosexuals are very much like everyone else is one of the keys in bringing our fears under management.

Another step in bringing our fears under control is the choice to love our homosexual brothers and sisters.

The writer of the Epistle of I John advises us, "There is no fear in love, but perfect love casts out fear; for fear has to do with punishment. . . ." (I John 4:18 NRSV). The validity of our choice to love our gay and lesbian friends will be confirmed by a subsiding of our fears.

Once we heterosexual Christians put our own house in order, we will be ready to meet and to be reconciled to these present day strangers. It is when homosexuals and heterosexuals meet on level ground without prejudice, that we discover how much alike we really are. We also find that sexuality is a very small slice of life.

When Marie began attending worship services, she came with a mutual friend I knew to be gay. At our first lunch, homosexuality was never mentioned. Her uppermost concern was her relationship to Christ and her membership in the family of God. We talked about Jesus and God's love. That conversation was unique because Marie is a unique person. It was also a very ordinary conversation not unlike conversations familiar to almost any pastor. We parted knowing the conversation had hardly begun. For our next appointment, Marie insisted that she provide lunch and asked that I come by her workplace.

When I arrived I had no idea what to expect. Marie

greeted me with a picnic basket in hand. She took me to her place of quiet and meditation. Her special place was a small park alongside Ship Creek. In the spring and summer, the viewer can watch various varieties of salmon head up the creek on their trip to their spawning grounds. Some fishing is allowed, and anglers can be watched casting for their prize. The shores of the creek are also a sometimes gathering point for wild ducks and geese. Marie had not only packed a lunch for the two of us, she had brought a bag of pieces of bread for the ducks. The lunch for Marie and me was homemade fried chicken, potato salad, rolls, a thermos of lemonade, and a homemade chocolate cake. We sat at the picnic table near the river and fed the ducks as we fed ourselves. This was Marie's sanctuary and she had invited me to join her in this special place.

In this setting to which we returned several times, Marie shared her struggles, anger, and frustration about her schizophrenic mother. What did all this emotional pain and misery have to do with God? Was God angry with her? Was God angry with her mother? Marie herself experienced extended periods of nagging depression. Was this the sins of the parent falling on a new generation?

In the process I shared one of my own pains. I, too, have a close family member who is schizophrenic. Mental illness became a part of our kinship. I could never say, "Marie, I know how you feel," but I could assure her that her own pain was one of the common denominators of life, that we have a Lord who participates in our pain and who will ultimately heal us all.

In my pastoral ministry with Marie, I learned that her life revolved around 1) her own struggle for survival, 2) her schizophrenic mother, and 3) her own bouts with depression. I also learned that her being lesbian, having been settled, was incidental to her life, not central.

One of the disservices that Christians and churches have done to gay men and lesbians is to make their sexual orientation of central importance. Among heterosexual persons we have long, important conversations about a whole array of subjects without any reference to sexuality. Is there any reason this should not be true as we relate to homosexual persons?

A lesbian, who has been in a heterosexual marriage, borne children, and finds herself a divorced, single parent head of household, faces a difficult and lonely road lying ahead. If she were heterosexual, we would all understand her desire for adult companionship, a new marriage, and the help of a partner in raising her children. We would even introduce her to men we feel might be interested in her. The lesbian in this circumstance has already learned by hard experience that a heterosexual marriage did not work and will not work for her. Understandably she looks not for a male companion but a female companion to find friendship, intimacy, and a parenting partnership. In this circumstance our lesbian mother does not ask questions of law or religious teaching. She may not even consider the question of public acceptance. Driven by the realities of her life, she starts the process of socializing and dating.

The scenario just described was the real-life circumstances of Dianne. Her daughter, Judy, was eight years old when Dianne met Hester. After dating, they decided to become a couple and moved in together. Hester had been reared Roman Catholic but had renounced the Catholic Church out of both feminist convictions and lesbian disenchantment. Her live-in relationship with Dianne was her first. Not only did she enjoy her relationship with Dianne, Hester also liked the family unit and her new parent relationship with Judy. For her, one element was missing. She wanted God's blessing on her new household.

Hester and Dianne invited me to be a part of their world. Setting aside the fact they were lesbian, working with them in preparation for their service of blessing was no different from working with a heterosexual couple. We talked about their commitments to each other and to Judy. We talked of the parenting dynamics. We talked about how they planned to handle

156

money and possessions. We planned the service and reviewed the promises they would be making to each other.

The service was held in the church's prayer chapel. The fifteen or so women who attended packed the small space. The service was solemn. The service was joyful. Their promises were sealed with rings. It ended with the traditional embrace and kiss, and they were introduced as a couple bound for life. The celebration moved to their apartment. Additional friends joined in the festivities. A friend had baked and decorated a cake. Guests brought gifts, and they were opened. It was a great, fun evening.

The union of Hester and Dianne and the celebration of that union obviously focused on the relationship of two lesbians. Looking past that fact, the dynamics were completely familiar to every minister and to every church. There was nothing sinister about their desires, motives, or intentions. Both Hester and Dianne wanted stability and opportunity for Judy. It seems to be very appropriate for the churches and their clergy to say, "God bless you."

As Cliff deteriorated with life-draining bouts with AIDS-related pneumonia, he became too weak to leave his home by himself. He had requested that he not be hospitalized. Art, his partner of many years, took care of him except when away at his job. Their circle of friends, mostly gay and lesbian, made sure his every need was met. For times when Cliff found breathing difficult, oxygen was kept at his bedside. There was almost always someone there with him. I visited him regularly, and Darlene sometimes joined me. Cliff was a fiber artist. He bought raw wool and spun it into yarn, and then knitted sweaters or wove tapestries.

Finally Cliff did not have the strength to leave his bed. He had spun and woven his last. Art's mother came from out of state to be of help. I cannot imagine a dying person being surrounded by a more loving cast.

On Saturday morning I received a call from Art. Cliff had requested a visit. I visited him that afternoon. Cliff had decided it was time to accept death. He knew the Gospel very well. I read Bible passages familiar to us both. "Even though I walk through the valley of the shadow of death, I will fear no evil." "For God so loved the world that he gave his only son that whoever believes in him might not perish but have eternal life." "There is therefore now no condemnation for those who are in Christ Jesus." "Who can separate us from the love of God?" "We are more than conquerors through him who loved us."

Then we sang hymns. He knew them as well as I did. We did not need a hymnal. His once strong, mellow baritone voice was now no more than a whisper.

"Naught have I gotten, but what I received,
Grace has bestowed it since I have believed.
Boasting excluded, pride I abase,
I'm only a sinner saved by grace."
        (Only a Sinner, James Gray and Daniel Towner)

"On a hill far away stood an old rugged cross,
The emblem of suffering and shame.
And I love that old cross where the dearest and best
For a world of lost sinners was slain.
So I'll cherish the old rugged cross,
Till my trophies at last I lay down.
I'll cling to the old rugged cross,
And exchange it some day for a crown."
        (The Old Rugged Cross, George Bennard)

"Amazing grace how sweet the sound
That saved a wretch like me.
I once was lost but now am found
Was blind but now I see."
        (Amazing Grace, John Newton)

With one last prayer of confession, claiming of the Gospel, and thanksgiving, I left.   Cliff asked that he be given no more oxygen.   He died early Sunday morning.

During his life Cliff kayaked Prince William Sound, hiked the hills and mountains of Alaska, bicycled the highways and trails of Alaska, Fiji, and New Zealand.   He was a member of the Audubon Society and the Anchorage Weavers and Spinners Guild.   He was a marvelous cook, a fine guitarist, and a baritone of real quality.   The fact that Cliff was gay seemed so irrelevant.

In all three illustrations, in real life situations, vital Christian ministry took place.   All the vital elements needed for ministry were present.   There was honesty.   Everyone involved accepted one another as the people we were.   There was trust.   Needs were shared, not hidden.   As a minister I had not only welcomed them, I had identified with them openly and publicly.

The final act that made ministry possible was the welcoming of a heterosexual pastor into their world.   Marie took me to her place of retreat alongside Ship Creek and fed me.   Hester and Dianne invited me to participate in solemnizing their most important human commitment and to their home to continue the celebration.   Cliff invited me to the side of his death bed.

If churches decided with honesty to welcome gay men and lesbians, they should not expect a rush of returning homosexuals or an explosion of new ministry.   The when and where of ministry will not be set by the churches.   Ministry will take place when homosexuals trust ministers and churches enough to invite them into their world.   Ministry will most likely take place on their territory, not the churches'.

Chapter 7

THE CHURCH'S MINISTRY TO HOMOSEXUAL TEENAGERS

The presence of homosexuals in our society is a fact. It is a fact of the past. It is a fact of the present. It is a fact of the future. The evidence says that same-sex orientation is biological and no more than incidentally environmental. If a person's sexual orientation is genetic, as is now widely held with scientific justification, the future presence of homosexuals among us is assured. Apparently homosexuality is a wide-based permanent part of the human gene pool. When recurrence of a phenomenon is long-term and produces no inherent physical, vocational, psychological, or sociologic impairment, labeling the phenomenon sickness, evil, or abnormal becomes increasingly difficult. This was the point when the American Psychiatric Association removed homosexuality from its list of mental illnesses. The continued condemnation of homosexuals, the persistence of homosexual myths, and pervasive homophobia say that basic information is not being provided to the general population; or at least when it is provided, it is not heard or is disbelieved.

Meanwhile the new generations of gay and lesbian persons are being born and proceeding through our families, schools, and churches toward adult homosexual life. According to Identity's *One in Ten* study some homosexuals are aware of their sexual orientation to the same sex by the time they enter grade school. The average age at which they are aware of their same-sex orientation is twelve and a half years. Translated into year in school, the typical homosexual person is aware of same-sex orientation in seventh grade. From there our typical soon-to-be teenager will go through eight years of absolute silence. Our homosexual teenager will not tell a friend, a sibling, a teacher, or any other human being the closely guarded secret. The teenage homosexual will hear the words queer, fairy, fag, and fruit, knowing full well who the despised one is. A more cruel dynamic cannot be imagined.

Yet there is no one who will provide teenage homosexuals with information about same-sex orientation.

Adult gay and lesbian leaders have developed an array of periodicals and printed materials for homosexual adults. However, no matter how much they would like to provide information and encouragement to gay teenagers, they do not dare. Public acceptance of the myth of homosexual recruitment is overpowering.

The realities of heterosexual perversions are well known and documented. The practice of perverted heterosexual sex is widespread. Heterosexuals participate in prostitution. They misuse minors in the production of pornography. They sexually abuse children. Heterosexuals prey on runaway teenagers. We all need to recognize that sexual perversion has nothing to do with sexual orientation. Both heterosexual and homosexuals can make perverted uses of their sexuality. Sex can be perverted and misused without regard to sexual orientation.

There are enough known cases of sexual abuse of minors by homosexuals to encourage a homophobic society to suspect all homosexuals of seducing and recruiting young people to homosexuality. That constant suspicion is unfair to all of the highly responsible homosexuals in our society. But the myth that young people are recruited into homosexuality by adult homosexuals is so strong that gay and lesbian adults do not dare talk to a teenage homosexual about sexual matters. No gay organization dares publish printed information designed to help gay and lesbian teenagers. In today's American society homosexuals or homophile organizations might well face some sort of legal action should they begin providing teenagers with any type of literature that would help them sort out their sexual orientation.

Every homosexual adult with whom I have raised the issue of teenage education about sexual orientation has agreed that such education is urgent. Not a single one is willing to participate in any way in an educational venture that involves teenage homosexuals. The personal risk is too great.

When I think of education, I think of schools. Many public schools have sex education classes as part of their regular curriculum. Naively, I suspect, I decided public schools were the logical place for sex orientation education. I talked to school administrators. Without exception, administrators agree there is a significant number of homosexual students in their schools. This is not debatable. They do not doubt the teenage homosexual's isolation and his or her need for accurate information about sexual orientation. Again no element of debate is present. Each one said that because of public opinion and pressure, nothing can be done. I suspect for the time being they are correct. The hands of public school administrators and teachers are tied by public ignorance, opinion, and prejudice.

Within my own denomination, American Baptist Churches USA, the tension over the place of homosexuals in the life of our churches is growing. Those churches that have been open to homosexuals are becoming more open in their public identification. The Association of Welcoming and Affirming Baptists has been formed. Some of these congregations have welcomed gay and lesbian members for years. Others have been sympathetic but more cautious and less open. They are being challenged to make their openness publicly known. The leaders of the movement have defined a welcoming and affirming church very minimally: "It means that a church is welcoming of gay men and lesbians, that it may be publicly listed as open and affirming, and that the congregation will help support the association."

If the new Association of Welcoming and Affirming Baptists and open churches of other denominations become truly serious about their responsibilities to gay and lesbian persons, they will find the path leads to more than public declarations. A commitment to gay and lesbian persons, if taken seriously, inevitably leads to a commitment to homosexual teenagers. They will need to address a task that the homosexual population and the public schools systematically avoid. The serious church must become specific and concrete about its ministry. It is not enough to care about teenage homosexuals in general.

Homosexual teenagers are very special. They live in constant fear. They are afraid of physical violence. They are afraid of rejection of family, peers, and church. They are afraid they will never be accepted as "normal" by society. They are very lonely. Statistics about teenage homosexuals are impossible to gather. If the generally accepted 10 percent is valid, that same 10 percent is a valid projection of the number of gay and lesbian students in our school systems. Beyond that, the statistics that we hear about the homosexual teenagers among us are projections by the adult homosexual population based on their own teenage experience. Following are some of the statements that are being made by homosexuals and that are generally accepted in homosexual circles:

- 30% of all teenage suicides are homosexuals.

- A high percentage, possibly as many as half, of teenage runaways are homosexual.

- A majority of homosexual teenagers are abusers of alcohol and drugs and make up a high percentage of all teenage alcohol and drug abusers.

- A high percentage of teen pregnancies involve lesbian girls trying to prove to themselves that they are "normal."

A high percentage of children and teens recruited into pornography and prostitution are homosexuals whose self esteem has been destroyed.

These are the projections of people who have gone through the harrowing experience of being a teenager and homosexual.

I have attended seminars on teenage suicide and teenage alcohol and drug abuse. Not one mention has been made of the homosexual factor. I have heard presentations about teenage runaways. No mention has been made of the homosexual factor. On those occasions when I have raised the issue, I have had one of two reactions: 1) "You do not know what you are talking about." 2) (in private) "I believe you are correct, but we cannot talk about it."

As my circle of homosexual friends has enlarged, and as I have listened and taken seriously their experience, I believe they are telling the approximate truth. They are our very best source of information, even though they can point to no scientific sociological research to verify their contentions.

If churches are serious about welcoming gay and lesbian teenagers, they face the fact that they are inviting some of our most disturbed and troubled kids, not because they are homosexual, but because they are rejected and condemned by category by an ignorant and hostile general population. If our churches are to be open and affirming toward homosexual teenagers, they must be prepared for the realities of their commitment. Our congregations, even those with the most welcoming history, have to be educated. Typical members of openminded and affirming churches are highly idealistic. When they say, "Everyone is welcome," they say the words honestly.

165

They are also ignorant of what they are saying.

The known facts about the same-sex orientation must be stated and discussed within the church body over and over again. We must do it redundantly until the facts are imbedded in our very being. Homosexuals do not choose their sexual orientation. Adult homosexuals do not recruit teenagers into homosexuality. Homosexuals are just as capable of being good parents as heterosexuals. Homosexuals want to live in commitment based on intimate relationships just as do heterosexuals. Homosexuals are just as capable of loving God and serving God as heterosexuals. There is no uncontested incompatibility between the teaching of the Bible and same-sex sexual orientation. If the members of an open and affirming church become convinced of these truths, they will be better prepared to accept and handle the criticism and slander that will surely come.

Within the church, teenage members especially need to be educated in the basic facts of homosexuality. They need to have an opportunity to sort out their feelings about association with known teenage homosexuals. There are some facts the Christian heterosexual teenager needs to know about their homosexual counterpart. They too want to date. They, too, want to go to social events coupled with a date to whom they're attracted. They, too, want to participate in all of the socializing processes that we associate with the teen years.

Openly accepting gay and lesbian teenagers into the life of our churches presents a testing field for the gospel itself. The gospel presents Christ as taking on the burden that is not his own. He takes on our burdens because the load is crushing and because he loves us and values us. The burden being heaped on homosexual teenagers is more than they can bear. They are being crushed. Paul sums up the Christian ethic with these words: "Bear one another's burdens, and in this way you will fulfill the law of Christ." (Galatians 6:2 NRSV) The bearing of the homosexual teenager's burden is a specific task of the open and affirming church. Accepting as our own the homosexual teenager's burden of isolation and rejection may well be the very heart of the church's responsibility.

Once the open and affirming church is committed to and educated about the teenage homosexual, specific actions can be taken. Before anything else is done, a body of literature has to be produced. Reading material is key because it can be read, reread, and digested in the teenage homosexual's privacy. Almost without exception the first real caring contact between an open and affirming church and an emotionally and socially imprisoned homosexual teenager will be a piece of reading material.

Computers, copiers, and all the elements of desk top publishing are marvelous tools at a church's disposal. Our churches have a great pool of writing skills, starting with their ministers. Usually local churches have depended on their denominational hierarchy to provide literature on a wide variety of subjects. This will not happen with literature aimed at the teenage homosexual. Homophile groups will not develop literature for use by churches. Their literature would always be suspect. Literature will of necessity be developed on the level of the local church.

Such literature will give the facts of the homosexual phenomenon in language that can be understood by teenagers. The literature will make a straightforward application of the gospel on the love of God in Christ. The literature will offer counsel that is understanding and caring. The literature will assure anonymity to anyone who might respond. The literature will offer a safe church home. The literature will offer a way to contact a helping person. The literature will identify author and church.

Distribution of such literature is where the true test of the open and affirming church begins. Literature can be kept very safely in the church literature rack. The whole exercise of deciding, educating, and writing is somewhat pointless unless the literature reaches every teenager in the community. Some professionals will be happy to have the printed resource for use in specific cases.   But in general the information will not be welcomed by a homophobic public. It will be welcomed by the teenage homosexual, but the church will not quickly hear from even the most appreciative teenager.

Earlier I commented that I have no idea what shape the open and affirming church may take. This is particularly true of the open and affirming youth group that is prepared to meet gay and lesbian teenagers in the context of a truly caring youth group. Whatever the change may be, I would expect it to be evolutionary rather than revolutionary and dramatic. In other words, nothing much that is obvious will change in the church. There will be some public outrage from those who hold differing opinions. That protest will soon subside, and still nothing much that is obvious will change in the church. There will be no rush of new teenage homosexuals into the church. The first eventual response will probably come from homosexual teenagers who are already in the church but hiding from the people who care the most. At that point teenage homosexuals and heterosexuals will start as friends to educate one another in an entirely different way.

As a pastor I have always found the initial positive response to a declared openness has been from homosexuals who are already in the church but tightly closeted. I have always been surprised by each disclosure. The educating, the discussions, the written materials, and the public avowal of acceptance are all very important. But it will be our gay and lesbian friends from within who will teach us the basic lessons and who will lead us down a more creative path.

If the adult gay and lesbian leaders are correct in their assessment of the role of gay and lesbian youth in the problems of suicide, alcoholism, drug addiction, runaways, prostitution, and teen pregnancies, the church that is informed and well prepared can become a major player in addressing these pressing problems. The church is always at its best when it is welcoming the fugitive, the sojourner, the stranger, the outcast. I have little confidence in the variety of institutional band-aids that are being offered by our society to our lost youth.   The church will be a faithful servant people when root problems are faced and long-term answers are provided.   The festering social sore of the closeted homosexual teenager is waiting to be addressed.   If churches do not address the reality, no one will in the foreseeable future.

There is always the fear that homosexuals will flood our churches and church programs if welcomed openly and honestly. My first reaction is, "So what!"   Even so, I doubt if it will happen. The traditions of our varied denominations are very precious and have great holding power for the homosexual who has been raised in the church.   As important as the Metropolitan Community Churches are in the gay movement for public acceptance, gay men and lesbians do not want to be part of a church based on sexual orientation.   Applying this same dynamic to our teenage homosexuals, they are not eagerly waiting to move to a Baptist church that is open and affirming.   They want to be accepted and affirmed in their own tradition.

The open and affirming congregation will not be a magnet drawing dozens of new gay and lesbian youth to their church and youth program.   More likely the open and affirming congregation will be salt that will flavor the whole community of churches. They will more likely be the leaven that will cause the Christian community to rise to new significance in the general population. They will more likely be the candle that can bring light into a very dark room.

Chapter 8

THE CHURCH'S MINISTRY TO HOMOSEXUAL FAMILIES

Bill is an ordained Lutheran minister who lives a part of his life in a closet. Is he homosexual? No, he is a happily married heterosexual. Does he have homosexual children? No, his children are too young for that fear or speculation. What part of Bill's life is closeted? His mother is lesbian, and he was raised by his mother and her lesbian lover.

Bill heard of my interest in bringing justice to our homosexual brothers and sisters. I knew him as just one of the Lutheran ministers in the community who participated in ecumenical activities. He invited me to lunch. The conversation began, "Howard, I have never shared this with anyone other than my wife."

Bill was born in Iowa. He has one sister two years older than he. Their mother was divorced when Bill was three. Bill does not remember his father. His mother and "Aunt Jane" along with the two children moved to California immediately after the divorce. Bill and his sister grew up in a household with two parents. Mother and Aunt Jane shared in the parenting responsibility. The household was stable and loving. Mother and Aunt Jane both worked outside the home. Both shared in the homemaking responsibilities. They purchased a home and lived in a nice middle-class neighborhood. Mother and Aunt Jane shared a bedroom and slept together.

As he grew up, Bill always felt free to invite friends to his house. It was perfectly normal to introduce his mother and Aunt Jane. When he reached high school, he followed the usual patterns of socializing and dating. He felt free to bring a girl friend to his home and introduce her to Mom and Aunt Jane.

171

In retrospect Bill never at any time experienced his growing up as being abnormal. He was never shortchanged on love and attention.

The church background of both Bill's mother and Aunt Jane was Lutheran. It was only natural when they moved to California for the family to become a part of a Lutheran church. Bill and his sister went to Sunday School, completed catechism, were confirmed, and were super-active in the youth group. As Bill looked back, he recognized that his mother and Aunt Jane were not totally active in the life of the church. They attended worship services regularly, but they did not participate in the social or organizational life of the church. They never became a part of any study groups or special interest groups.

During the years of growing up in his family home, Bill was almost totally unaware of homosexuality. As he was about to leave for college, his mother approached him about the need for an extended conversation. For the first time she explained that she was lesbian and that Aunt Jane was her lesbian lover. She explained the social patterns that were carefully planned to keep her and Aunt Jane closeted and to keep Bill and his sister from suffering any undue stigma. At no time during college and seminary did Bill share the family secret with anyone other than his wife, whom he married in his middle year in seminary.

When Bill faced oral examination for his ordination, he was concerned about answering questions about his family background. At the time there was dissentious debate among seminary students and faculty about the ordination of homosexuals. While he was not homosexual, his convictions were clear. He saw his mother as a virtuous woman. He saw the relationship between his mother and Aunt Jane as loving and wholesome. He saw nothing about their relationship worthy of condemnation. He had concluded that the blessing of a relationship like that of his mother and Aunt Jane was completely justified. He resented that his mother had felt that

172

she must hide her most important chosen human relationship from the church. Apparently his marriage was enough to discourage the raising of any questions about homosexuality. He was relieved. But his deep feelings about his family and his convictions about the church and homosexuals remain as deeply closeted as is the typical homosexual person.

Is Bill's family unusual? Not really. Today, families headed by homosexuals abound. From their learned skill of hiding, homosexuals have developed an ability to keep a low family profile. These new-style families go unnoticed by the undiscerning eye.

The forming of families by homosexuals is not surprising, if one reflects on their situation. All homosexuals have grown up in some sort of family. Whether the family was stable or unstable, caring or cold, one parent or two, two generations or three, is not at issue. They all grow up in a family. Because they have grown up in families, family is just as natural to the homosexual as it is to the heterosexual. The isolation that comes following their awareness of same-sex sexual orientation is experienced as a threat to family. They fear rejection by everyone, but especially by family. The journey of the homosexual can aptly be described as a search for family.

Among heterosexual young people the dating process is a movement toward eventual establishment of family. The dating process is not easy for anyone and has many pitfalls. But the heterosexual young person somehow survives the dating process, finds a mate, and establishes a family. Few heterosexual people want to end up single. Few heterosexual people want to end up childless. Family is natural to them.

Homosexuals have exactly the same drive for family. They want to be coupled with a person of their choice whom they love. They want to be parents.

Because a woman is lesbian does not mean she has any less desire to be pregnant, to give birth to a child of her own, and to rear that child with the help of a mate. Because a man is gay does not mean he has no desire to be a father. He wants to cradle a child of his own in his arms. He, too, wants to take a son fishing and to help a daughter with her math and eventually escort her down the marriage aisle.

It is the drive for family that has led so many homosexuals into marriage with heterosexuals. They assumed it was their only chance to have family. This assumption is now being challenged. Twenty-five years of concerted effort toward gay liberation has opened new opportunities for gay men and lesbians to initiate families with new patterns.

The pattern of Bill's family is one of the most frequent. A lesbian has entered a heterosexual marriage. She bears children, but for a multiplicity of reasons, the marriage fails. Through the experience of marriage, the lesbian is convinced of the irrevocable nature of her sexual orientation. She seeks female companionship and eventually enters a long-term, same-sex relationship. She has either primary custody or shared custody of her children. The two-parent homosexual family like Bill's is formed.

Lesbian couples have found additional ways of adding children to their household. Women who are perceived to be single have been able to adopt children, especially children who are difficult to place. This often results in adoptions of children who may be racially different, handicapped in some way, or advanced in age. The adoption, in reality, is not by a single woman but by a lesbian couple.

A method of adding children to a lesbian household that is growing immensely in popularity is artificial insemination. Today a person can select the sperm of a biological father from a catalog. Want a biological father who is 6'3" tall, 195 pounds, dark hair, brown eyes, and an IQ of 135? It can be arranged. This is the wave of the future among many lesbians. With the new openness, with an abundance of information, with the support of rapidly growing lesbian organizations, fewer and fewer lesbians will see a heterosexual marriage as their only opportunity for bearing and rearing children.

Yet another pattern is emerging. The idea that gay men do not enjoy female companions or that lesbians do not enjoy male companions is not true. Gay men and lesbians regularly socialize with one another, but not romantically. Lesbian couples and gay couples socialize. Out of such friendships have developed another homosexual family pattern. A lesbian couple and a gay couple who are close friends will enter into a parenting arrangement. Children are conceived and then an ongoing parenting agreement is worked out between the two households.

Gay couples are also forming households that include children. Many times the children come from an earlier, unsuccessful heterosexual marriage. Adoptions are more difficult for gay men than for lesbians, but they do occur. There is also a growing incidence of gay couples making arrangements with surrogate mothers to bear children for them.

Another type of homosexual family is the most hidden from public view. It is the family in which mother or father is homosexual and who for whatever reason has decided to remain in the heterosexual marriage. Such families are easily accepted in society because no one knows. However, ministers need to be aware that such families exist because they may well end up in their pastor's office seeking counsel and help.

Too often we think family is a valid term only when children are present in the household. A couple bound together by promises is also a family.

The homosexual couple is an expression of the basic desire for family. The dominant public prejudice is that homosexuals are interested in one another for sex only. Sex is no more dominant in a gay or lesbian relationship than in a heterosexual relationship. The dominant themes in a gay or

175

lesbian union are the same as in a heterosexual union. The dominant themes are companionship, caring, sharing, giving, and receiving. The heterosexual couple is generally accepted as a family for good reason. So also ought gay and lesbian couples be recognized as families.

Our society has made it difficult for homosexuals to form families. Churches have been a part of the resistance. Churches have been reluctant to broaden or change their definition of family. Thirty years ago churches were struggling to know what to do with the single parent and blended families that began to appear. Divorced men and women, and especially divorced and remarried men and women, were routinely excluded from holding office in many churches. A divorced minister became unemployable, and when he decided to remarry, he knew it meant a change in profession as well. Today even the most conservative denominations ordain and keep in good standing ministers who have been divorced and remarried. Church boards are filled with members who are single divorced parents, single never-married parents, and divorced and remarried adults who lead blended families. The acceptance of non-conforming families was forced by sheer weight of numbers of failed and reconstituted families. Now churches are going to face the challenge of further broadening their definition of family to include the developing array of homosexual families.

Certain phrases send a message to gay families. A church that treasures "traditional family values" or advertises itself as "a family church" is sending homosexual families a message to stay away. Still other churches send a stay-away message by their silence. In the future, increasing pressure will be put on churches to declare themselves in some way. The silence cannot continue because of the sheer weight of numbers. Homosexual families will become too numerous to be ignored.

Gay men and lesbians certainly are individuals, but their unique individuality cannot be understood and appreciated apart from their family life and commitments. Almost every homosexual I know either is living as a part of a family or has the goal of forming a family. There is no way for churches to minister effectively with the gay and lesbian population without ministering to their families.

There was a day when churches could avoid facing their full responsibility to the homosexual population. As long as gay men and lesbians merely attend worship services as individuals and draw no particular attention to themselves, they blend in. Gay families do not blend in so readily. Avoiding responsibilities becomes more difficult.

The dilemma can be illustrated by baptism of infants and small children. Almost every church practices the baptism of infants. Those who do not regularly hold some sort of dedication or welcoming service for infants and small children. Every such service calls for the involvement of parents. As gay families form in growing numbers, will churches take down the welcome sign for the children of homosexuals? Will churches refuse to baptize a child with two same-sex parent-partners participating and with a same-sex couple standing with them as Godparents?

The issue of children may eventually be one of the powerful forces to bring about inclusion of homosexual families in the life of the church. Churches have always recognized that the building of the future of the church lies in the provision of programs for children. Many churches deliberately and effectively use children's programs as a way to recruit parents and other family members. Sunday School, children's choir, play days and outings, puppet programs, performances, and attendance awards all can be justified in and of themselves. But every minister knows all these programs need the cooperation of parents. Will the children of homosexual households be welcomed? The number of homosexual families is growing and will grow dramatically in the future. Just as the volume of divorces forced a change of attitude in the churches, so also the volume of homosexual families will surely force a change of attitude toward their presence in the churches.

On those occasions when Darlene and I visit our children, there is no more tender experience than attending a worship service and receiving communion as a family. In those settings I do not receive communion simply as an individual believer. I receive the bread and the wine with my family as a communal act. I am not alone in that experience. For many families communion celebration is a regular act of binding family together as well as binding family to God. Gay families want no less experience. Gay and lesbian couples want to come to the communion rail hand in hand and in the company of their children. They want no less than the spiritual opportunities afforded to other couples and families.

This brings us to a central issue: The blessing of gay and lesbian couples. I do not care to involve myself in the question of legal recognition of same-sex marriages. I am willing to leave that question in the hands of Caesar. The issue before churches is the bringing of God's joy and happiness to a same-sex couple. The key issues need to be reviewed.

For the homosexual, sexual attraction to someone of the same sex is normal and natural. This attraction is just as normal to the homosexual as a heterosexual's attraction to someone of the opposite sex. Such attraction is not chosen, and there is no sustained evidence that same-sex attraction can be changed in the homosexual.

Sexual expression for homosexuals can be either responsible or irresponsible. Some forms of homosexual expression can be both unwise and physically harmful. The same is true of heterosexual sexual expression. Sexual expression by homosexuals can take place in committed relationships or it can be blatantly promiscuous. The same is true of heterosexual sexual expression.

Homosexuals enter into long-term, monogamous relationships out of wholesome desire and high idealism. They seek companionship, stability, intimacy, mutual support, and opportunity for family. Their motivation matches the highest motivations of heterosexual couples.

As an American Baptist minister, I do not officiate at marriages under any restraints or direction from a hierarchy. I am fully free to claim God's blessing on any couple that might come to me. I have only one firm requirement. I ask enough of the couple's time to become acquainted with them. I have one basic concern. I want to have a chance to discover the intent of the couple.

When I have been asked to officiate at same-sex holy unions, I have tried to bring exactly the same concerns to the homosexual couple as I have to the heterosexual couple. As I plan to bring God's blessing to a gay or lesbian couple, I want to have an opportunity to discover their intent. Every same-sex couple for whom I have been the officiant at a service of holy union has had the same desires, motivations, and intents as their heterosexual counterparts. I have found no reason to withhold God's blessing from homosexuals who sincerely want their relationship to be a holy union.

In looking at the dynamics of gay and lesbian families, I have tried to understand the experience of children growing up with two same-sex parents. Much is made of the absence of adequate role models in single-parent households. How does a boy learn to be a man in a household led by two women? How does a girl learn to be a woman in a household led by two men? We again find ourselves operating in new territory without surveys, studies, or research. We are in the early stages of a new phenomenon with no substantial number of products of such households to study. In trying to understand the dynamics of families headed by homosexual couples, I talked with a professional counselor who is gay and a personal friend. He suggested I was concerned about the wrong thing and was asking the wrong questions.

My friend believes the family is only one of the many sources for role modeling for the growing and developing child. A typical child has an abundant exposure to a wide range of role models. Every child is exposed to teachers, coaches, Sunday School teachers, neighbors, ministers, etc. I understood what he meant because, even today, I draw on models of coaches, teachers, ministers, and professors from my past. My friend, Bill, with whom I began this essay about homosexual families, is a good example. He was raised by his mother and Aunt Jane. He had no contact with his father from the time he was three. Yet he shows no sign of identity confusion. He is thoroughly masculine in appearance and movement. He is happily married to a delightfully feminine woman. He is interested in sports and other activities which are considered masculine. He relates comfortably with both men and women.

My gay counselor friend maintains the key to heathy homes is not gender but genuine, honest love. A child who is loved during the growing up process will be secure and perfectly able to sort through the role models offered in our society. The household led by two people with commitments of love to each other is prepared to love children. My counselor friend believes the mature gay or lesbian couple is just as able to love children wholesomely as a heterosexual couple. I suspect he is correct.

In a 1976 interview, then presidential candidate Jimmy Carter was asked his opinions about homosexuality. He responded, "The issue of homosexuality always makes me nervous." The interviewer asked if his response was for political reasons. Carter continued, "No, it's more complicated than that. It's political, it's moral, and it's strange territory for me."

I respect the moral discussion about homosexuality which must take place among us. But I believe it is the "strange territory" element that makes us most uneasy. I respect the concern of some people about the rearing of children in gay and lesbian households.   But I believe the greatest problems in sorting out our understanding is that the majority population is uneasy because we know we are in territory that is strange and unknown to us.

What better place for homosexual and heterosexual families to get to know one another than in the life of the church?   Being open and affirming means more than singing together, praying together, and celebrating communion together. Bill's mother and Aunt Jane should be blessed, included in study groups, parenting classes, potlucks, and picnics.   They should be seen, accepted, and treated as the couple with family they, in fact, are.   Seems strange?   Only so long as we are hesitant to be truly open and affirming.

Chapter 9

THE CHURCH'S MINISTRY TO AFFECTED HETEROSEXUALS

For every gay or lesbian person there are two disturbed, possibly heartbroken parents. Parents hope for a daughter or a son. But a homosexual child of either sex? Please, no! I have never met a parent who was overjoyed when a son or a daughter made homosexual orientation known. In fact, hearing the news is a terrible blow, even if already suspected. Parents are not the only persons sent into a state of trauma. Brothers, sisters, grandparents, and close family friends are all deeply affected when they hear the news.

The most likely response of parents, other family members, and friends is silence. It is a silence born of fear: fear for their child, sibling, or friend—fear for themselves. There has been little opportunity for knowledge and understanding. The information generally available about the homosexual phenomenon is very negative. The language used in common conversation is derogatory. The hostile language is just as intimidating to family and friends as it is to the gay man or lesbian. The family and friends of homosexuals, having heard the unwelcome news, go into the closet, close the door and even lock it. Their closet is just as rigid and dark as that of their homosexual sons, daughters, and friends. This particular group is huge. It is obviously much larger than the homosexual population itself. While the typical homosexual stays in the closet for an average of eight years, the typical parent, brother, sister, or friend stays in the closet for a lifetime. Even after two parents are aware, the subject is never a matter of discussion or conversation between them. Gay sons and lesbian daughters

183

bring welcome relief to their parents and family when they move from home and find a hometown of their own in a distant city.

Churches, when at their best, form a caring support system for hurting people.   As a pastor I have watched congregations perform marvelously well with hurting people. When a member is seriously ill, hospital visits are made, food is provided, special prayers are made. Congregations are especially adept at caring for families when a death has occurred.   When a family decides that funeral or memorial service should be held at the church, rather than at a funeral chapel, musicians, ushers, and pallbearers all rush to help. Church members are willing to go to great lengths to make the time of grieving more bearable. If childcare is needed, it is provided.   Food?   Church people take care of it.   Every need is covered—transportation, housing for out-of-town family, friendship during the terminal illness and friendship for family following the death.

Churches are even more caring when a death is especially tragic.   Traumatic deaths from accidents, suicides, or Sudden Infant Death Syndrome bring out the best in a congregation. Over and over, I have watched congregations fulfill the Bible's command to bear one another's burdens.   I have been justifiably proud.

Churches, after some struggle, are doing a commendable job with troubled families, troubled marriages, and divorced men and women.   Almost all churches have some sort of family and marriage enrichment program.   They have personal growth groups, mothers' clubs, and study groups. The typical seminary-trained pastor has had some good-quality training as a counselor. Some churches even have full-time professional counselors on their staff.

My point in reviewing some of the things churches do very well is to affirm my contention that the support performance of churches is quite good.   Churches are doing much more than holding Sunday School classes and worship services on Sunday.   No church is perfect, but almost all churches do a fine job in many areas.

Churches also have some notable failures on their record. The largest failure of the churches in America over the past vcentury is their inept handling of heavy drinkers and alcoholics. American Protestantism has not been able to say anything more creative than "Don't." Women were encouraged to join the Women's Christian Temperance Union, and preachers were expected to preach sermons calling for total abstinence. In the meantime the alcoholic found no help in churches. So a system of groups was devised called Alcoholics Anonymous.   Here alcoholics find understanding, support, and encouragement just as they should have received in churches. As thankful as I am for AA, the very existence of AA is an embarrassment to churches and a painful reminder that churches were too slow in developing an understanding of alcoholism and never created a framework of ministry to this large segment of our population. Ideally, if churches had responded with effective ministry, AA should not exist. But it does, and I am thankful for every person who finds sobriety in an AA group.

This describes my feelings about the existence of Metropolitan Community Churches. Ideally they should not be. They stand as a constant reminder that churches have been too slow in responding to the spiritual needs of gay men and lesbians.

When speaking about ministry to those who are not gay or lesbian but who are deeply affected, note has to be made of Parents and Friends of Lesbians and Gays, or P-FLAG for short. It is a relatively young organization, just thirteen years old.

In 1979 a Human Rights March on Washington was held. Parents of homosexual sons and daughters from across the country met for the first time. They found real help and strength from the friendships that were formed. In 1982 the Federation of Parents and Friends of Lesbians and Gays was

185

formed with twenty chapters. Thirteen years later P-FLAG is made up of over 350 chapters. The organization has chapters or key contacts in all fifty states and in several foreign countries. P-FLAG sponsors an ever-growing annual convention, and provides encouragement to tens of thousands of parents of gay men and lesbians.

P-FLAG has a five-point statement of purposes and objectives:

1. To provide a support system for families and friends of lesbians and gays in their effort to understand, accept, and support gays and lesbians with love and pride.

2. To offer support and understanding to gay and lesbian people.

3. To provide education for individuals and the public on the nature of homosexuality.

4. To support the full human and civil rights of lesbians and gays.

5. To speak out and act whenever necessary to defend and enhance those human and civil rights.

P-FLAG is one more organization that ideally should not exist. But it does, and I am thankful. Nevertheless, P-FLAG will always be a reminder to the churches of a job that is being left undone.

P-FLAG is a fact. It serves a need that is found in every community. For churches that want to begin caring for the needs of family and friends of gay and lesbian persons, a good start is to sponsor a chapter of P-FLAG for the community.[27]

Many chapters are already church sponsored. It will meet some real needs, not just of people in the sponsoring church, but of a broad range of churched and unchurched people in the community.

The church that sponsors a chapter of P-FLAG will not find the task difficult if a committed nucleus is available. Three or four parents are enough to begin. A small continuing ad in the PERSONALS section of the Classified Advertising section of the local newspaper will slowly produce additional people. The placing of brochures in the offices of sympathetic doctors, lawyers, and counselors will also bring responses from interested parents and friends. Sponsorship of a P-FLAG chapter should not be seen as a way to add members to the church roster. Sponsorship is a ministry. It is an extended hand of friendship and understanding.

Churches can do much more for parents and friends of homosexuals than sponsor a P-FLAG chapter. Whatever is done, church leaders must remember that the people to whom the church is extending a hand of friendship are deeply closeted. They are not sure they ever want to come out of the closet. Their reluctance to come out of the closet will be significant.

At the head of the list of things to be done by a church is the provision of reading material. The lack of reading material was mentioned in relation to homosexual teenagers. Now the subject reappears. Reading material is so very important to people who are closeted because of homosexuality. Reading is one thing closeted persons can do. They do not feel free to inquire, discuss, or argue, but they will read. The supply of reading material, especially from a Christian perspective, is in very short supply. I regularly read several Christian journals and magazines. I scan the book reviews and follow new publications of the religious publishing houses. I look in vain for books on the subject of homosexuality and the practice of the Christian faith. There are no books. There are no curricula being published by church bodies and their publishing arms. When I urge people to read; unfortunately, there is little to recommend.

The Paper that I first wrote and kept rewriting illustrates the hunger for reading material. *The Paper* was not a great piece of scholarship. As I read it now, I find it rather dull. *The Paper* dealt with psychological, sociological, theological, and biblical issues. There were no stories about the people who are affected by homosexuality.   There was no excitement, no emotion to the document.   My only publishing tools were a typewriter and a copier. I never, ever pushed *The Paper*. It was just there for interested people.   The response was clearly beyond what *The Paper* deserved.

Pastors and local churches need to become involved in producing and distributing reading materials. There is not just an argument to be made, there is a story to be told. The story of every gay man and lesbian is moving and has the potential of convincing a reader even when the best arguments are turned aside. Printing, distributing, telling, and retelling facts about the homosexual phenomenon convinces only a few. It is true that the person who has the facts has the advantage in any discussion, and people involved in the cause of justice for gay men and lesbians should always have their facts in hand.   However, we must have more to present than the facts.   We must tell the story.

In the past homosexuals have been hurt by the stories told about them. Because of stories, not facts, the public image of homosexual men has been presented as sex-crazed deviants who go to bed with hundreds of different men every year. The bath house has been presented as the center of gay lifestyle, and the gay bar has been presented as a den of iniquity at which gay men find their trick for the night.   The story of millions of loving, responsible, faithful gay and lesbian couples has never been told. I no longer tolerate bizarre stories of gay men and lesbians to be told in my presence.   I am armed with a full repertoire of stories about healthy, happy, productive homosexuals.

Parents have a particular story to tell. It is the story of their gay sons and lesbian daughters, their sons-in-law and daughters-in-law, and their grandchildren. It is also a story of their own struggle toward understanding, acceptance, and support. The story of every parent who has successfully come to grips with a son's or daughter's homosexuality needs to be recorded and shared. No one is in a better position to record these stories and to distribute them than the churches.

People in general want to be religious. People want a base of meaning for their lives that goes beyond biology, sociology, behavioral psychology, and statistical analysis. Most people find it impossible to go through life without, at some point, asking, "Why am I here?" "What is life all about?" Homosexuals want to be no less religious than the general public. Their desire to be religious is shown dramatically by the gay men and lesbians who remain in the churches despite despicable treatment. Likewise parents and friends of gays and lesbians are trying to understand homosexuality in the context of religious belief.

Any kind of sexuality is a difficult subject for Christian theology. Christians find difficulty in thinking of God, our Heavenly Father, in sexual terms. Even though we as Christians insist on a full humanity for Jesus Christ, we have never felt free to think of our Lord in sexual terms. Somehow the idea that Jesus was just as sexual as the rest of humanity troubles us. To suggest that Jesus had sexual desires just like our own seems almost blasphemous. Did Jesus go through the same psycho-sexual development process as does the rest of humanity? How could he be human and not?

The parents of gay men and lesbians are forced to think about their children's sexuality in theological terms. They have no choice. They have been forced by society to think of their children primarily in sexual terms.   Acceptance or rejection, salvation or condemnation, righteousness or sinfulness are being determined in the public eye and in the churches on the basis of their child's sexual orientation.   As they search for understanding, it is difficult to believe that answers will come from a God who is asexual; Jesus of Nazareth, who never had a sexual thought; a minister who is afraid to talk about faith and sexuality; or from congregations that never discuss such subjects. It is much safer to hold a Bible study and follow the three missionary journeys of the Apostle Paul. The one in four of our families that has a homosexual member needs to hear how homosexuality fits in the plan of God.

In 1978 James B. Nelson published his book *Embodiment*.[28] It is the best theological treatment of sexuality that I have read.   In the process of writing this present manuscript, I returned to Nelson's work and reread it.   His message is even more timely now than it was in 1978. Probably 1978 was a time too early for the book to get a fair hearing. Churches were not yet in the sexual crisis in which they now find themselves. Now that Christian churches and denominations of all stripes are heading into full crisis situations because of the subject of homosexuality, possibly Nelson can be more appreciated.

Embodiment looks at sexuality through theological eyes. The history of Christian attitudes is reviewed.   The book is written in a gracious manner. It is not a polemic. While Nelson makes his own views plain, he leaves room for new understandings and even for disagreement. Of the ten chapters of the book, one is devoted to homosexuality and the issues that face the church.

In his review of contemporary attitudes of Christians towards homosexuals, he first identifies the "rejecting-punitive" orientation. This position, though it is not held by any major contemporary theologian, is popularly held by many Christians.

It is based on uninformed literal interpretations of the Old Testament purity codes and in its most severe form calls for the death penalty for any homosexual activity. The second position is called "rejecting-nonpunitive." It is most widely held in the Roman Catholic Church. It is based on homosexuality's unnaturalness. Homosexual expression does not contribute to the procreation of children. All homosexual activities are confessional sins. While homosexual orientation is not a sin to be confessed, it is never to be expressed. Celibacy is the only acceptable behavior.

"Qualified acceptance" is the third position identified by Nelson. From this point of view homosexuality is a perversion of the fundamental order of creation. Homosexuality is a part of the basic "fallenness" of creation and should be viewed in that context. It is acknowledged that homosexuality is not chosen. In effect the gay or lesbian person is told that their plight is not unlike a person born blind, retarded, or deaf. According to this view, Christians sympathize with the homosexual's plight, but what they are experiencing is the product of the fall and is not part of the will of God. God's grace is with the gay man or lesbian. By grace the homosexual is accepted in the Christian community but as a cripple.

The fourth theological possibility is "full acceptance." From this point of view, same-sex sexual orientation is not only seen as a given, it is a gift from God with full blessing. Homosexual orientation can lead to selfless affection just as can heterosexual orientation. Overt homosexual expression can be a wholesome expression of the same love with which God has loved the world through his son, Jesus Christ.

From the beginning of my personal journey, I never considered the first two possible positions. There was no way I could square rejection with the gospel I had come to love. During the early years of my journey, I embraced the third possibility, "qualified acceptance." I was sure that the grace of

God was broad enough and deep enough that gay men and lesbians could be regular participating members of a Christian community. My attitude was that the church was made up of people who regularly confessed their sins. Every member had enough history of flaws and failures so that stone throwing had to be renounced. Eventually, however, observing gay and lesbian couples who loved one another dearly, I was forced to drop "qualified" and adopt "full."

I remain a Christian with what most would identify as somewhat conservative beliefs. However, I now firmly believe that the family of God is more diverse than I once thought. I believe God's creation is marked by diversity rather than conformity. I believe homosexual orientation and responsible homosexual expression are just as much a part of the will of God as heterosexual orientation and heterosexual expression.

The parents, families, and friends of gay men and lesbians need to hear this message. They need to read this message in materials produced by their church.

This brings us to another key part of the churches' ministry to the circle of people affected by the homosexual phenomenon. It is well illustrated by a conversation that took place between me and another pastor. My pastor friend was noticeably pleased with himself as he shared how he had handled a conversation with a young gay man who had come to him with the pain of his homosexuality. The pastor had listened with compassion. The young man had not been involved in any overt homosexual activity. However, he had come to the conclusion that he was gay and felt terribly guilty. He was afraid of God's rejection and condemnation. After listening to him, my friend spoke to him about God's forgiveness in Christ and assured him of God's grace. He prayed with the young man and sent him on his way.

My reaction was one of anger and was not at first understood by my friend. I was upset because he had claimed

Christ's forgiveness for a person who had done nothing wrong. He had assured a person of God's grace for something for which he was not responsible. He had not even suggested it was all right to be who he was. All he had done was set the young man up for another round of guilt.

The almost universal first question of the parent of a gay son or lesbian daughter is, "What did I do wrong?" The appropriate answer is, "Nothing." To address the person with God's forgiveness and grace is to affirm that the parent has indeed done something wrong.

Feelings of guilt should play a positive role in our lives, not a negative one. The ability to feel guilty is a precious gift from God. In a practical way, guilt is to moral life what pain is to physical life. No one enjoys pain, but it serves a useful function because it tells a person when something has gone wrong in the physical body. Pain leads to diagnosis and treatment. No one could live a normal life without the ability to feel pain. Likewise guilt, generated by conscience, is a signal to morally sensitive people that something is wrong. Healthy guilt does not debilitate a person; rather it calls a person to initiate corrective action. When corrective action is taken, guilt subsides. But what happens when a person feels guilty and nothing, in fact, is wrong? This is a very common dilemma that a pastor is often called upon to address.

Americans in general are a morally concerned people. American society has trained its people to feel guilty. Americans can become a guilt-driven people. Who is responsible? I have heard Puritan Protestantism blamed. I have heard Methodists blamed. I have heard Roman Catholics blamed. I have heard blame placed on our adversarial legal system. No matter how the guilt-ridden American society is to be explained, it is a reality. Sometimes Americans feel guilty for things for which they are indeed responsible. Other times Americans feel terribly guilty for things for which they have no responsibility.

For example, in America today there are millions of people who feel responsible for their parent's alcoholism. The guilt they feel shapes their lives even though there is no rationale by which responsibility can be placed on a child for the alcoholism of a parent. Meetings for Adult Children of Alcoholics enjoy very good attendance. People are there trying to be relieved of the guilt they have assumed for no good reason.

The parents of homosexual children suffer in much the same way. Their lives become guilt driven. They live with their guilt in a closet. Their perception is that something is going wrong. Tragedy is taking place. Someone must be responsible. Parents take on the responsibility and feel terribly guilty for something they cannot explain and that they do not understand. What has happened has nothing to do with the parenting they have done. They have done nothing that has caused their child's sexual orientation. Even though most parents in this situation will not come out of the closet to talk with their pastor, the knowledgeable pastor must make an effort to extend information and affirmation, not forgiveness in the name of Christ.

A major responsibility of pastors and churches is to define those things for which a person should experience guilt and those things for which a person should not experience guilt. Such ministry is an exercise in the training of conscience. One in every four families has a homosexual family member. Churches are allowing the world and high-profile fundamentalists to train the conscience of the congregation. There is no reason for gay men and lesbians to feel guilty about their sexual orientation. There is no reason for parents of a gay son or lesbian daughter to feel guilty for some imagined determining role. It is the job of pastors and churches to make this message heard.

One last question. How do pastors either draw family and friends out of their closet or gain entrance to their closet? It is never acceptable to take a gay man, lesbian or their family members out of their closets.   Ideally they should all come out, all the way out.   But that is not going to happen in the near future.   All closeted persons have their reasons to be in the closet.   Those reasons have to be respected.   The first way to penetrate the closet door is by providing reading materials.   The second is from the pulpit and in the classroom.

The third way to gain entrance to someone's closet is to be an intruder.   Ministers do not like being an intruder. Ministers feel more confident when a parishioner calls to make an appointment.   The minister is then working in familiar territory.   An intruding ministry is consistent with the gospel itself.   God did not send his son following an invitation from the world.   Jesus Christ was and is an intruder.   During his years of earthly ministry Jesus went many places where he had no invitation.   He was aggressive in recruiting his disciples.   He raised questions other people did not dare ask.   There are times when ministers should go places where not invited and raise questions others dare not raise.   Over the years I have confronted people about heavy drinking, marital infidelity, public policy, personal beliefs, child-rearing practices, and many other circumstances where I felt injustice, wrongdoing, or error was involved. And I have initiated conversations with parents of gays and lesbians.

I have always tried to be discreet when initiating conversations with these parents.   I have always tried to give information.   I have intruded to offer an understanding ear.   I have intruded to encourage reconciliation with a son or daughter.   I have intruded to enlist support for the cause of justice for homosexuals. I have intruded to suggest it was time to leave the closet.

Success rate?   Not high.   Bringing ministry to such a tightly closeted group will always be a low-percentage exercise. What positive results occur are usually delayed months or even years.

There will always be plenty of pastors and churches willing to do the popular tasks of ministry. Without diminishing their value, Sunday School teachers, church musicians, and youth sponsors do not meet much resistance to their ministries. Churches need to balance their popular ministries with unpopular and difficult ministries. Putting together a sensitive, aggressive ministry to the parents and friends of gay men and lesbians is one of the unpopular and difficult ministries that needs to be initiated.

Chapter 10

THE MINISTRY OF ADVOCACY

The Hebrew and Christian traditions have always carried a strong commitment to the doing of social justice. Among the Hebrew prophets the doing of justice was a central demand. The Mosaic code called for the appointment of judges to ensure justice. The code commanded, "You shall not distort justice, and you must not sow partiality. . . . Justice and only justice, you shall pursue. . . ." (Deuteronomy 16:19, 20 NRSV).

The book of Psalms is full of references to God's love of justice. In the Isaiah and Jeremiah writings, justice and righteousness are presented as inseparable twins. The prophet Amos makes an impassioned plea "But let justice roll down like waters, and righteousness like an ever flowing stream." (Amos 5:24 NRSV).

The Hebrew commitment to justice is eloquently summarized by the prophet Micah. "And what does the Lord require of you but to do justice, and to love kindness, and to walk humbly with your God." (Micah 6:8 NRSV).

This central message of justice found throughout the Hebrew tradition was powerfully embraced by Jesus of Nazareth. Jesus's Sermon on the Mount did not call for anything that he did not find in Moses, Isaiah, and Jeremiah. The Sermon on the Mount can rightfully be called the new demand for justice. A central charge Jesus made against the religious establishment of his day was that they ". . . neglect justice and the love of God. . ." (Luke 11:42 NRSV). For this neglect he pronounced woes on the perpetrators.

Some Christian churches have been marvelous champions of the causes of justice. Some have shamefully neglected the Bible's demand for justice. Most churches have been a mixed bag of commitment and neglect. Even those who have attempted to be faithful to the call of justice have been selective at times of the neighbors who are to receive justice. It has not been uncommon to screen those who are to receive justice according to race, sex, economics, education, age, religion, or nationality. At one time or another, however, churches have been willing to lead society's demands for justice.

My own denomination has a distinguished history of demanding justice for various groups. It is one of the reasons that I have felt so proud of my denomination over my lifetime.

An example of the activities of American Baptists in the pursuit of justice is our Office of Governmental Relations in Washington, DC. On the agenda of the OGR are military spending, energy, housing, federal budget priorities, the death penalty, civil rights, the Middle East, health care, Haitian refugees, discrimination against women, and accommodations for disabled persons. The OGR staff does an excellent job keeping Baptists informed and involved and keeping legislators informed of the justice issues that concern their constituency.

The concern for justice that is illustrated by the American Baptist Office of Governmental Relations runs through the entire denomination. American Baptist concern for justice runs through our foreign and home mission programs, our evangelism, and our educational ministries. Justice concerns have very deep roots in our local American Baptist congregations.

Yet few understand the dismay of a few American Baptists who are distraught over the current debate in the denomination about whether or not homosexuals should be welcomed in our churches. At the same time American Baptists are demanding justice for a broad array of citizens, not a word is being said about the horrors of discrimination against the homosexual population.

What is true of American Baptists is also true of every major Christian body in America. Not only is there a silence on the subject of justice for our gay and lesbian neighbors, churches have become a major contributor to injustice.

I never dreamed of the level of injustice against homosexuals until they became my friends. The findings in Identity's *One in Ten* study reveal a horror of discrimination.[29]

71% of the respondents had experienced some form of discrimination.

58% had been verbally abused because of their sexual orientation.

24% had received threats of violence.

14% had been followed or chased.

12% had experienced damage to their property.

11% had experienced physical violence.

8% reported police harassment.

4% had been forced to move because of their sexual orientation.

11% reported difficulty being hired because of their sexual orientation.

35% reported problems while on the job because of sexual orientation.

8% had been fired from at least one job because of sexual orientation.

Hiding is the only way gay men and lesbians have found to avoid even more discrimination.

When Christians claim justice for humanity, they typically

do not require those for whom they have become advocates to meet some level of righteousness. For instance, when Christians protest the use of the death penalty, they do not raise questions of the guilt or innocence of the persons involved. Homosexuals are the only identifiable group Christians apparently deem unworthy of justice.

In the decades since the Stonewall Inn incident little progress has been made in establishing civil rights for gay men and lesbians. Eight states and the District of Columbia have passed legislation assuring civil rights for homosexuals. That leaves 42 states to go. At least 65 cities and 17 counties have done the same. But thousands more need to follow. In most of America, homosexuals have no legal protection against discrimination because of their sexual orientation. In the few instances where their civil rights have gained protection, churches have played no significant role in gaining the victory. In fact, churches have led the fight in many areas to deny the granting of civil protections for homosexuals.

The persecution of homosexuals by the U.S. military is a national disgrace and illustrates our national attitude. Several years ago when a disastrous explosion took place on the USS Iowa, the Naval Investigative Service concocted a lurid story about Clayton Hartwig, one of the 47 sailors who died in the explosion. He supposedly had a "special relationship" with Kendall Truitt who was the beneficiary of Hartwig's $100,000 life insurance policy. There was never a shred of evidence that Hartwig or Truitt was gay. But military homophobia made it the perfect ploy to divert attention from evidence that the likely reason for the explosion was gunpowder that had destabilized as a result of improper storage conditions.

Gay men and lesbians regularly serve in the U.S. military with honor. They do so only because they work very hard at staying in their closets. U.S. military policy about homosexuals had been official and plainly stated. It was clearly stated by then Secretary of Defense Casper Weinberger in 1982.

According to Weinberger homosexuality is incompatible with military service.

> The presence of such members adversely affects the ability of the Armed Forces to maintain discipline, good order, and morale; to foster mutual trust and confidence among the members; to ensure the integrity of the system of rank and command; to facilitate assignment and worldwide deployment of members who frequently must live and work under close conditions affording minimal privacy; to recruit and retain members of the military services; to maintain the public acceptablilty of the military services; and, in certain circumstances, to prevent breeches of security.

There is no evidence any of the preceding is true except "to maintain the public acceptability of the military services." This is particularly difficult to address. Gays were unacceptable because they were unacceptable. This was exactly the same argument that was used to keep the military racially segregated prior to 1948. At that time racial integration of the military was unacceptable. Harry Truman changed that by executive order. Now with a fully integrated military, we see clearly how silly segregation was. Yet the nation continues discrimination toward homosexuals for the same silly reasons.

Incidents of persecution of gay men and lesbians keep recurring in the Army, Navy, Marines, Air Force, and Coast Guard. The patterns of persecution recur. Under this policy no evidence was required. The military system was police, legal counsel, judge, and jury. In a directive in 1982, the Pentagon broadened the definition of homosexuality, the basis of exclusions, to include, "A person who engages in, desires to engage in or intends to engage in homosexual acts." In other words, homosexuals could be dismissed from military service not for anything they have done but for what they think and feel.

The injustices to homosexuals in the U.S. military are

numerous and well-documented. Yet there was no concerted protest except by gay and lesbian activists. The silence of churches is especially disillusioning. Spotted owls and darter fish draw more demands for justice.

The 1992 Presidential election campaign brought hope to gay men and lesbians as candidate Bill Clinton embraced justice for them in the nation's military. When Clinton was elected, many expected an order from the Commander-in-Chief barring discrimination against homosexuals in the military just as Harry Truman ended racial discrimination in 1948. But homophobia won over justice. A policy of "Don't ask, don't tell" was adopted as a compromise. While some overt aggressive persecution has been thwarted, the deadly dynamic of the closet has been enhanced. Justice for gay men and lesbians in the U.S. military has not been achieved under President Clinton.

The gay and lesbian population is very limited in fighting for their own justice. So many of them are hidden and have a perceived need to remain closeted. To carry their own protest would take them out of their closets. It is a Catch 22. The homosexuals that feel free to lead the protest against injustice are seen as radical activists and the effects are often marginal. Of all groups that live with overt and persistent injustice, homosexuals are most in need of a champion to carry their need for justice.

I believe there is substantial support in the churches for justice for the gay and lesbian population. Understandably, potential advocates of justice are afraid to be open. They are as closeted as the gay and lesbian population itself. They have a perceived need to remain closeted. To come out of their closets will assign them to the same injustice suffered by their despised gay and lesbian counterparts.

Deciding to be an active advocate for gay and lesbian justice is very much like experiencing conversion. It hinges on a decision, a commitment. It dictates a new course of action. It takes a person into unfamiliar territory. It is too dramatic to be hidden. It is inevitably misunderstood by many.

Injustice to homosexuals will remain entrenched until Christians in sufficient number become public advocates of justice for all. For those who want to become active advocates, concrete actions need to be taken. Here are some suggestions:

Never Allow a Derogatory Remark About Homosexuals to go Unchallenged

We all hear degrading and false statements about gays and lesbians. We hear the words fag, fairy, and queer. Every unkind word should be challenged. A kind but direct challenge can actually bring creative conversation. I have observed parents of a gay son or a lesbian daughter sitting through painful conversations. A simple response like "You are speaking of someone's son, and I am offended" would have been appropriate and ultimately helpful.

Never Allow a Distorted News Story, Opinion Column, or Letter to the Editor to go Unchallenged

Become a writer of letters to the editor yourself. Too often, flagrantly false items are printed. They will be accepted by a homophobic and uncritical public if they are not thoughtfully challenged. Other politically active groups have put together organizations solely for the purpose of writing letters to the editor to ensure a hearing for their particular point of view or cause. Such action makes sense for all of us who are committed to justice for gays and lesbians.

Appear at Public Discussions and Speak on Behalf of Gays and Lesbians

Legislative bodies, committees, and commissions at all levels of government hold public hearings. Whenever justice for homosexuals is involved, directly or indirectly, Christians should be on hand to make statements on behalf of the rights and needs of gay men and lesbians. Sympathetic public officials (and there are some) will welcome the supportive comments. Statements of support keep the record straight and are helpful to public servants at every level.

Ask All Candidates for Public Office About Their Commitments to Justice for All, Including Homosexuals

Politicians are very sensitive to constituents, especially at election time. They will know how people feel about justice for homosexuals only if people speak up. I would never suggest judging candidates on a single issue; however, when a question is asked, a candidate is put on notice that justice for homosexuals is an issue that cannot be avoided.

Appear Before the Local School Board and Inform the Board of the Presence of Gay and Lesbian Students and the Implications of That Presence

Typical school board meetings allow opportunity for public input. Take advantage of the opportunity. Many school board members and school administrators are not aware of what is happening to their most hidden student minority. Awareness is the first step toward justice. School officials need to know of community support for our homosexual kids. They are in need of just treatment.

Join Gay and Lesbian Organizations in Public Events

Gay Pride parades are the most prominent public events sponsored by gay organizations. They are often the only public activity in which various gay and lesbian organizations cooperate with one another. The parades are in the spring and commemorate the Stonewall Inn uprising. Marching with our gay and lesbian friends is encouraging to them and is a way to begin establishing a relationship of trust with them. Picnics are also becoming popular. While their purpose is to bring gay men and lesbians together in a large public event, they are also an opportunity for heterosexuals to become personally acquainted with their gay and lesbian neighbors. Heterosexuals will find themselves very welcome.

Ministers Can Make Friends with the Pastor of the Local Metropolitan Community Church and Sponsor Their New Friend into the Local Ministerial Alliance or Fellowship

The typical pastor of a Metropolitan Community Church is an educated, well-trained, articulate, caring professional person. The general clergy population needs to make the acquaintance of their gay and lesbian cohorts. It won't happen unless someone takes the initiative to do the introducing.

Homosexuals, Their Families, Their Parents, and Their Friends Who Do Not Feel Free to Come out of the Closet to the Public Should Consider Coming out to Their Pastor so That the Pastor Can Better Understand the Realities

The typical minister has no idea of the web of lies in the ordinary congregation. Almost all ministers are very conscientious about keeping the secrets of parishioners. It is only when affected persons share with pastors that pastors are forced to deal with issues in personal terms rather than by faceless categories. This is a huge step in the education of ministers.

Local situations call for particular actions. Injustice has many faces. We need to accept the challenge of confronting every one of those faces. Public calls for justice will be tailored to each of those faces in their local setting. An informed person who is committed to the doing of justice on behalf of the homosexual population will know what to do. Just do it!

> Let justice roll down like waters. (Amos 5:24 NRSV)

> And what does the Lord require of you but to do justice, and to love kindness, and to walk humbly with your God."   (Micah 6:8 NRSV)

Chapter 11

THE WOUNDED HEALER

One of the surprises in pastoral ministry is the way in which the helped becomes the helper, the enemy becomes the friend, the despised becomes the savior, and the wounded becomes the healer. I say it is a surprise, but it should not be. It is so much a part of our Bible tradition and Christian belief.

I do not recall when I was first drawn to the Old Testament story of Joseph. It was probably during those grade school years when a child's most persistent complaint is, "But Mom, that's not fair!" I do know that as an adult I never tire of the story. Joseph is unusual in that a negative word is never said about him. If he ever complained, it is not reported. If he were ever bitter, it was not recorded. He was despised by his brothers, and he was the object of jealousy, but not a single negative response is ever assigned to him. His brothers sold him into Egyptian slavery. Joseph worked responsibly as a slave of Potiphar, an Egyptian Army captain. Potiphar's wife falsely accused him of attempted rape. He was thrown into prison. In prison he correctly interpreted the dream of Pharaoh's chief butler who had fallen from the favor of Pharaoh. When the chief butler was restored to his position, he forgot Joseph. Joseph sat in prison for two more years. When he was finally released from his unjust imprisonment, he worked as a highly valued servant of the Pharaoh himself. From that position he became the savior of his family including his brothers who had despised him and sold him into slavery.

When Joseph revealed himself to his brothers, his grace was magnanimous. "I am your brother, Joseph, whom you sold into Egypt. And do not be distressed or angry with yourselves because you sold me here; for God sent me before you to preserve life." (Genesis 45:4,5 NRSV).

In the Bible the tradition of the despised savior begins with Joseph.

The writer of the Isaiah prophecy could well have been borrowing from the experience of Joseph when he wrote "He was despised, and we esteemed him not. Surely he has borne our griefs and carried our sorrows." (Isaiah 53:3,4 NRSV).

The setting of Isaiah 53 is generally accepted to be the Babylonian captivity. It was written by disciples of Isaiah rather than the Eighth Century BC prophet himself.

Fewer than 5,000 Israelites lived in Babylonia, the city of their exile. They were the Israelites who had survived the holocaust of conquests that wiped first the Northern Kingdom and then Judah from the map. The city of Jerusalem and the cherished temple built by Solomon had been destroyed and the land was controlled by an alien foreign nation. The restoration of the throne of David was hardly imaginable. In that setting the Isaiah writer found a reason for the existence of the small remnant of God's people. The new Israel was to be God's servant to the world. In Chapter 53, one twist to the servitude was added. The servant of God was to be a suffering servant. Out of wounds, rejection, and sorrow, not by military power, Israel was to become a savior nation. Israel was to bear the griefs, sorrows, and transgressions of others and thus to be their savior. The iniquity of all was to be laid upon the suffering servant. The suffering servant was to be a sin offering by which many are to be accounted righteous.

Jesus of Nazareth embraced the servant dynamics of Isaiah with a passion. Not only did he embrace the servant model, he embraced the suffering-servant ideal for his own ministry. For the past two thousand years, Christians have read the words of Isaiah 53 and have viewed Jesus of Nazareth hanging on the cross.

He was despised and rejected by others;
 a man of suffering and acquainted with infirmity;
and as one from whom others hide their faces
 he was despised, and we held him of no account.

Surely he has borne our infirmities
 and carried our diseases;
yet we accounted him stricken,
 struck down by God, and afflicted.
But he was wounded for our transgressions,
 crushed for our iniquities;
upon him was the punishment that made us whole,
 and by his bruises we are healed.
All we like sheep have gone astray;
 we have all turned to our own way,
and the LORD has laid on him the iniquity of us all.

He was oppressed and he was afflicted,
 yet he did not open his mouth;
like a lamb that is led to the slaughter,
 and like a sheep that before its shearers is silent,
 so he did not open his mouth.
By a perversion of justice he was taken away.
 Who could have imagined his future?
For he was cut off from the land of the living,
 stricken for the transgression of my people.
They made his grave with the wicked
 and his tomb with the rich,
although he had done no violence,
 and there was no deceit in his mouth.

Yet it was the will of the LORD to crush him with
 pain.
When you make his life an offering for sin,
 he shall see his offspring, and shall prolong his days;
through him the will of the LORD shall prosper.

(Isaiah 53:3-10 NRSV)

Henri J.M. Nouwen has become a very important modern-day commentator on the spiritual life. Articles from his authorship are recurring fare in journals such as *The New Oxford Review* and *Sojourners*. Whenever I see his name, I am eager to see what spiritual insights he might have for me. Nothing Nouwen has written has touched me quite like his *Wounded Healer*.[30] The book is a series of four essays about pastoral ministry. The fourth essay is the key. It is entitled "Ministry by a Lonely Minister" with a subtitle "The Wounded Healer."

Nouwen maintains that loneliness is the hallmark of pastoral ministry. It is also a description of our mobile, rootless society. Whether we call it alienation or separation or isolation or loneliness, it is the deepest wound of our society. As Nouwen describes the personal loneliness of the minister, I knew he was talking about me. In my thirty-six years of pastoral ministry, I have never felt anyone has understood me. No one has understood the swirl of my inner emotions and motivations. I doubt if anyone can understand the intensity of my anger toward injustice, the depth of my honest caring, or the obscenity of my indifference. Being convinced that no one understands me and believing few even care, I am inevitably left a deeply wounded person.

My parents did not understand me as the adult I became. Knowing me probably would have been overwhelming to them. My brothers and sisters do not understand me. The roads I have chosen to travel are strange to them, and the reasons I have chosen those paths would be a mystery to them. My children care about me, but I accept that as they choose paths of their own, I will be more and more of a stranger to them. My wife loves me dearly, and I am devoted to her almost to absurdity. She understands me only somewhat. I fear if she knew me fully, she would flee in terror. I doubt if anyone would stay in my vicinity if they knew me. I am the wounded minister of whom Nouwen speaks. He is correct in his analysis that my deepest wound is my loneliness.

As I have pondered this loneliness, occasionally I have rejoiced in my loneliness. Sometimes I laugh at its folly. Other times I sit down and cry over the intensity of its hurt. There are times I want people to know me. Other times I cherish my loneliness because it makes me who I am. Sometimes I dare to believe my loneliness is the genius of God.

It is this strain of painful loneliness that marks the people of God. Can you imagine the loneliness of Joseph as he was led off into Egyptian slavery? There was no one who could have understood his anger and frustration over the false accusation of attempted rape. He was in absolute loneliness as he sat in prison another two years when Pharaoh's butler conveniently forgot him. Joseph's wounds were especially painful because they were inflicted on him by people who should have cared. But his wounds of loneliness were what made him who he was.

The Isaiah writer saw Israel in this same lonely, painful, wounded dilemma. He had the profound insight to understand that the deep wounds of their isolation in a strange and unwelcoming land held the highest possibility of service to God.

Jesus of Nazareth walked the earth for thirty-three years. Three of those years were spent in intense ministry of teaching and preaching. He gathered twelve disciples around him. He taught them at length and in depth. Yet there is no evidence that this circle of close friends had the foggiest notion of who he was or what he was about. They had dumb discussions when he was not present, fell asleep when he prayed, stayed at a distance when he was tried, and ran in panic when he was crucified. I suspect Jesus's deepest wound was not from nails or swords but from loneliness that was caused by his own unfathomable purpose. How else do we explain his cry, "My God, my God, why have you forsaken me?"

And I am reminded that it is by his wounds that I am

211

healed.

I believe I have been a better pastor because of my wounds initiated by loneliness. I know I have had my share of failures, but I also know I have brought healing to many. In retrospect, I became a better pastor once I accepted my loneliness rather than seeking a solution for it. I now see my wounds from loneliness as a gift from God that is never to be relieved by marriage, family, or a congregation.

Nouwen suggests that ministers are truly prepared for ministry when they feel at home in their own houses with loneliness and wounds that are still present. It is then that ministers are prepared to offer hospitality to the most unexpected guest. The minister's attention can be given to the guest because it is no longer focused on personal wounds. Nouwen sees hospitality as the key act of ministry. He defines hospitality as the "ability to pay attention to the guest."[31] This is impossible if a minister's attention in any sense is still on internalized injuries. When a minister truly pays attention to the guest, ministry takes place. The guest is healed and salvation is known.

What does this have to do with ministry to homosexuals? I have reread Nouwen's essay at least a dozen times. It is generously highlighted and underlined. I have kept *Wounded Healer* beside my bed and have taken many short glimpses at its pages before closing my eyes. I have read it with me in mind. I have also read it with the gay and lesbian population in mind.

My first observation is of the church's ministry to homosexual persons. I suspect that few ministers come to terms with the central Christian theme of servant ministry. Rather than seeking greatness that comes from being the servant of all, we prefer the places of honor that are accorded to other professional persons in the community who have an educational level similar to our own. We become success seekers and define success by numbers, size, prestige, and neighborhood.

In a seminary homiletics class, the professor told us, "I will guarantee a church of 1,500 members within twenty years for anyone who will master the art of preaching." The challenge was very appealing to young ministers who were filled with ambition to succeed. I have never doubted the truth of my professor's statement. But there was no professor who warned me and my seminary colleagues of the loneliness that is intrinsic to the Christian ministry and the inevitable wounds that come from that loneliness.

In yet another class I was taught the techniques of Carl Roger's client-centered counseling. I was excited about the possibilities of helping people through counseling. But somehow I missed the suffering servant ideal for ministry. No one explained that I would be able to hear a guest in my office only if I had accepted my own wounds and cherished them, not for display but for their enabling power for me as a pastor.

If a stranger comes to the door of a minister and the minister is preoccupied with claiming the world's success, there is no room for the stranger. The stranger leaves still a stranger and takes her wounds with her. Ministers who attain popularity and success do not address the basic loneliness of life or the added loneliness of ministry.

They have only complicated their dilemma and become even more lonely. Having never embraced a servant ideal for ministry, ministers are not prepared to find ministry in the wounds of loneliness. The stranger again comes to their doors, and there is still no room because they are preoccupied with their own wounds. The stranger leaves still a stranger and takes his wounds with him.

In our society, gay men and lesbians are the ultimate strangers. We are happily insensitive to their loneliness, though they live next door. Too often we ministers are not at home in our own house of wounds. Homosexual strangers are the last people we want to show up at our doors. We are preoccupied with other things. We have no room for them. We reason they will bring trouble if we welcome them. We cannot give our attention to them because our attention is directed at being successful or much too often at our wounds from loneliness. We send them away and find reasons to justify our rejection.

But this is a very persistent bunch of strangers. While some move on and never return to our door, there is always a new crop that is growing up in our families, congregations and communities. Homosexuals keep coming to the minister's door. I keep wondering if we will ever be at home enough in our own house that we can say, "Welcome. We have reserved a place for you. May we have the privilege of hearing your story?"

My second observation is of the potential of the homosexual's ministry to the church. This potential first struck me when reading Nouwen's comments about loneliness being the source of one of our most painful wounds. Every homosexual person I have known has had profound experience with loneliness.

In our understanding of gay men and lesbians we must always begin with the period of time that begins with the first awareness of same-sex orientation and concludes with the first sharing of this fact with another human being. This is a period of time that averages eight years. It is an eight-year period that is dominated by intense fear and searching introspection. During this period that covers the teen years, young homosexuals ponder the worth of life. They deal with discrimination, insult, threat, and intense loneliness. Most contemplate suicide but choose life.

Even after this extended period of lonely silence is broken, young homosexuals are very selective with whom they share anything of real importance. Many never share their sexual discovery with parents or family. The dynamic of the closet develops and homosexuals become very calculating about the select individuals to whom the door of their closet will ever be opened. Alienation, separation, and isolation do their work, and loneliness becomes all-encompassing.

My first impulse is to say to the person who is homosexual, "Let me be your friend. Let me take away your loneliness and heal your wound." That would be most unchristian to do. As Nouwen points out: "No love or friendship, no intimate embrace or tender kiss, no community, commune or collective, no man or woman, will ever be able to satisfy our desire to be released from our lonely condition."[32] The gospel speaks a truth that no one, including the homosexual person, wants to hear. *Accept your loneliness as a gift from God, embrace your wound and come, join in the healing of humankind.*

Reflect back on the experience of Joseph. His life was a horror of injustice that surely produced the wounds of loneliness. But at the crucial hour of healing and salvation, Joseph knew his wounds were a gift from God for the saving of his family. Look back at the life of our Lord Jesus. He was misunderstood, deserted, unjustly accused, and cruelly killed. Yet we all confess that it was the will of God, for by his wounds we are healed.

The people of God always need a healer, a Messiah who will speak of peace and bring justice. We need a redeemer who will cleanse us from our hatred and oppressive ways. Deliverance for the people of God often comes to them in unexpected times and from unexpected places. Joseph was a surprise to his brothers. Jesus from Nazareth was a surprise to the world.

Could it be that the homosexual, obedient to the will of God, might be the church's modern day healer-messiah? Gay and lesbian believers fit the description. They are despised and rejected. They suffer and are acquainted with infirmity. They are rejected by a perversion of justice and cut off from the body of Christ. Is it possible that the will of the Lord will prosper through them?

PART II   Homosexuals, the Church, and Ministry

I have shared earlier that my experience with the gay and lesbian population has been heavily weighted by those with sincere religious intent. I do not suggest that the following description is a true picture of all homosexuals. But many of my gay and lesbian friends have come to terms with their wounds, accepted them, and found peace. Quietly they are building households in which they feel at home. They are not unhappy, unfulfilled, guilt-ridden wretches struggling to survive as some critics would have us believe. Over and over I have been impressed by their maturity attained against formidable obstacles. I find them living lives enriched by the performing arts, softball, music, politics, photography, community service, tasteful decor, social concerns, and healthy religious pursuits.

I began my faltering ministry with gay and lesbian friends by making sure they knew they were welcome at any church I pastored. They were welcome to attend, welcome to the membership, welcome to the offices of the church, and welcome to all the ministries of the church. Then in certain instances the relationship took a new turn. I was invited into their world.

Ken and Brad had bought a new home in South Anchorage. Darlene and I were pleased to receive an invitation to their open house. It was a large home with high ceilings and a marvelous view. The home had a formal dining room. A deck with access from both living room and dining room made the home seem even more spacious. The furnishings were coordinated in fine style. It all showed a touch of class and good taste. But the most rewarding part of the event for me was the privilege of meeting Ken and Brad's closest friends on their territory. Most were gay or lesbian, some were coupled. There were also some heterosexual couples present who obviously were at home in the setting.

Upon reflection I realized that we had been extended a truly magnanimous welcome. We had been welcomed not just into the home of gay friends, we had been welcomed into the world of gay friends.

I know the stories of both Ken and Brad. The stories are tales of rejection, fear, and loneliness. If any bitterness was left in either of them, they never spoke of it. They had accepted their wounds and had become Christian gentlemen. They had done more than acquire a fine house. They had created a home in which they felt completely at ease. They were so much at home they could make room for me, a heterosexual Baptist minister. I was blessed.

The church and the minister who are willing to embrace the suffering servant model of ministry will intentionally make room for our gay and lesbian friends. But I hope the interaction will not stop there. I pray our gay and lesbian friends will go a second mile with those of us who have caused their deepest wounds. Not just a few will accept the invitation. It may be that by the wounds suffered by our gay and lesbian friends many will be healed, restored, and made righteous.

NOTES

1. Edmond Bergler, *Homosexuality: Disease or Way of Life?* (New York: Collier, 1956).

2. Troy Perry, *The Lord Is My Shepherd and He Knows I'm Gay* (1972).

3. Ralph Blair, *An Evangelical Look at Homosexuality* (New York: Evangelicals Concerned, 1977).

4. Daniel Cappon, *Toward an Understanding of Homosexuality* (Englewood Cliffs, NJ: Prentice-Hall, 1965) p. 252.

5. Ibid. p. 252.

6. Jay Brause, et al., *One in Ten* (Anchorage: Identity, Inc., 1986).

7. Jay Brause and Melissa Green, *Identity Reports, Sexual Orientation Bias in Alaska* (Anchorage: Identity, Inc. 1989).

8. Troy Perry, op. cit.

9. John J. McNeil, *The Church and the Homosexual* (Boston, Beacon Press, 1976).

10. Letha Scanzoni and Virginia Ramey Mollenkott, *Is the Homosexual My Neighbor? Another Christian View* (Harper and Row, 1978).

11. A more extended list of gay organizations follows:
Affirmation (Mormons)
Affirmation (United Methodists)
American Baptists Concerned
Axios (Eastern and Orthodox Christian Gay Men
     and Women)
Brethren/Mennonite Council for Lesbian and Gay
     Concerns
Buddhist Association of the Gay and Lesbian
     Community
Christian Lesbians Out Together
Conference for Catholic Lesbians
Dignity, Inc. (Roman Catholic)
Emergence International (Christian Scientists)
Evangelicals Concerned
Evangelicals Together
Friends for Lesbian/Gay Concerns (Quaker)
Gay, Lesbian and Affirming Disciples (Disciples of
     Christ)
Integrity, Inc. (Episcopal)
Lifeline, Inc. (all Baptists)
Lutherans Concerned
National Gay Pentecostal Alliance
New Ways Ministry (Roman Catholic)
Nicheren Association (Buddhist)
Presbyterians for Lesbian/Gay Concerns
Reformed Church in America Gay Caucus
Seventh Day Adventist Kinship International
Sovereignty (Jehovah's Witnesses)
Unitarian Universalist Office for Lesbian and Gay
     Concerns
United Church Coalition for Lesbian/Gay
     Concerns
United Lesbian and Gay Christian Scientists
Universal Fellowship of Metropolitan Community
     Churches

Wingspan, St. Paul Reformation Lutheran Church
World Congress of Lesbian and Gay Jewish Organizations

Addresses for all the above organizations can be obtained from P-FLAG, 1012 14th Street NW, Washington, DC 20005.

12.   Alfred C. Kinsey, Wardell B. Pomeroy, and Clyde E. Martin. *Sexual Behaviour in the Human Male* (Philadelphia: W.B. Saunders, 1948).
Alfred C. Kinsey, Wardell B. Pomeroy, Clyde E. Martin, and Paul H. Gebhard. *Sexual Behaviour in the Human Female*. (Philadelphia: W.B. Saunders, 1963).

13.   Alan P. Bell and Martin S. Weinberg. *Homosexualities* (New York: Simon and Schuster, 1978).

14.   Robin Scroggs, *The New Testament and Homosexuality* (Philadelphia: Fortress Press, 1983).

15.   L. William Countryman, *Dirt, Greed, and Sex* (Philadelphia: Fortress Press, 1988).

16.   John Boswell, *Christianity, Social Tolerance, and Homosexuality* (Chicago: University of Chicago Press, 1980).

17.   John Boswell, *Same Sex Unions in Premodern Europe* (Villard, 1994).

18.   Alan P. Bell and Martin S. Weinberg op. cit., 53ff.

19.   Ibid. 27.

20.   Ibid. 30.

21. Robin Scroggs, op. cit.

22. Jay Brause et al.

23. Alfred C. Kinsey, Wardell B. Pomeroy, and Clyde E. Martin, op. cit.

25. Jeannine Gramick, et al., *Homosexuality in the Priesthood and the Religious Life* (New York: Crossroad Publishing, 1989).

26. Martin Marty, *Context* (March 1992).

27. Information about P-FLAG may be obtained by writing to P-FLAG, 1012 14th Street NW, Washington, DC 20005.

28. James B. Nelson, *Embodiment* (Minneapolis, MN Augsberg Publishing House, 1978).

29. Jay Brause, et al., op. cit. 4.

30. Henri J.M. Nouwen, *The Wounded Healer* (Garden City, NY Image Books, 1979).

31. Ibid. 90.

32. Ibid. 84.